Planet Earth

25 Environmental Projects You Can Build Yourself

Kathleen M. Reilly

Nomad Press

A division of Nomad Communications

10 9 8 7 6 5 4 3 2 1

ISBN: 978-1-9346700-4-0

Questions regarding the ordering of this book should be addressed to
Independent Publishers Group
814 N. Franklin St.
Chicago, IL 60610
www.ipgbook.com

Nomad Press
2456 Christian St.
White River Junction, VT 05001

green press
INITIATIVE

Nomad Press is committed to preserving ancient forests and natural resources. We elected to print *Planet Earth: 25 Environmental Projects You Can Build Yourself* on 100% postconsumer recycled paper, processed chlorine free. As a result, for this printing, we have saved:

Tree(s): 39
Solid Waste: 2,499 lb
Water: 23,588 gal
Suspended particles in the water: 15.8 lb
Air Emissions: 5,488 lb
Natural Gas: 5,719 ft^3

It's the equivalent of:

Tree(s): 0.8 american football field(s)
Water: a shower of 5.0 day(s)
Air Emissions: emissions of 0.5 car(s) per year

Nomad Press made this paper choice because our printer, McNaughton and Gunn, is a member of Green Press Initiative, a nonprofit program dedicated to supporting authors, publishers, and suppliers in their efforts to reduce their use of fiber obtained from endangered forests.

For more information, visit www.greenpressinitiative.org

ENVIRONMENTAL CHOICE · CHOIX ENVIRONNEMENTAL

BIO GAS ENERGY

FSC
Recycled
Supporting responsible use of forest resources
Cert no. SW-COC-002283
www.fsc.org
© 1996 Forest Stewardship Council

Other titles from Nomad Press

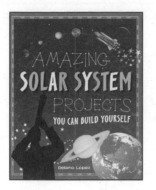

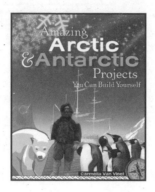

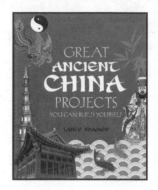

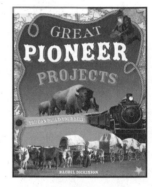

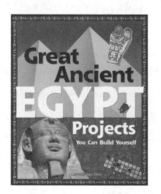

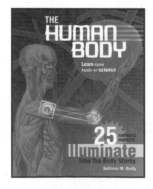

Contents

Introduction
Planet Earth: Our Ecosystem 1

Early Environmentalists

Henry David Thoreau (1817–1862) was a naturalist and philosopher who tried to live a simple life off the land.

John Muir (1838–1914), the "Father of Our National Parks," was one of the first preservationists. Muir believed in keeping natural areas untouched.

Theodore Roosevelt (1858–1919) was the 26th president, but he also was passionate about the outdoors. He created the first national bird preserve—and was the last trained observer of the passenger pigeon before its extinction. President Roosevelt designated many of our national monuments, including Muir Woods and the Grand Canyon.

Aldo Leopold (1887–1948) was considered the father of wildlife management; he founded The Wilderness Society.

Rachel Carson (1907–1964) was a biologist who wrote *Silent Spring*, a book that had a major impact on the way people looked at the environment.

Jacques-Yves Cousteau (1910–1997) was an underwater explorer who introduced sea life to people with his films and cared about the protection of the marine world.

James Lovelock (1919–) suggested that Earth is a whole, living organism, which he called the "Gaia" hypothesis.

Edward Abbey (1927–1989) wrote *Desert Solitaire* and was an outspoken environmentalist.

Major Organizations Protecting the Environment

Conservation International, seeks to demonstrate that human societies will thrive when in balance with nature.

Earthwatch Institute, brings science to life for people concerned about the Earth's future.

National Wildlife Federation, seeks to inspire Americans to protect wildlife for their children's future.

World Wide Fund for Nature, protects wildlife and the natural environment around the globe.

Nature Conservancy, works to protect ecologically important lands and waters for nature and people.

Sierra Club, is America's oldest and largest grassroots environmental organization, protecting communities and the planet.

The Wilderness Society, protects wilderness and inspires Americans to care for our wild places.

Planet Earth
Our Ecosystem

What's the world like outside your window? A grassy backyard, full of trees? Maybe some swaying palm trees or pine trees brush gently against your window at night. Or maybe there aren't any trees—but dry, desert air drifts in through your window. Maybe pigeons gather on your window ledge, far above the urban streets below.

Whatever you see out your window—that's the **environment**. Everything natural that's out there, living and nonliving, is what people are talking about when they say "the environment." The plants, like grass and trees; the animals, like birds, bugs, and bears; the rain falling; the sun shining down—even you. You're part of the environment, too.

1

It's nature, the world around us, the world that existed before the first human invention was even a dream. It's the things you can see—like critters and rocks and water—and things you can't see, like earthworms pushing through the ground under your feet and the air that's hugging you right now. And what's really neat to know is that all these elements, all these parts, are connected somehow, working together to create what we call the environment. Talk about teamwork!

Imagine the environment like an heirloom blanket, knitted from different pieces of yarn by someone a very long time ago. When it's whole, you can snuggle in its comfort. But if a thread is pulled, an entire section of your blanket can unravel—unless you catch it in time, that is. When you hear people talking about the environment lately, they're probably talking about the overall health of the earth, because more often now than in the past, scientists are studying the impact people have on the environment. They're studying how our habits, behaviors, and inventions are affecting the natural world.

And those scientists and people who care about the environment don't always agree about what's going on. Some believe the state of the environment is worse than ever, while others believe that it's part of a natural cycle. Some believe certain extinctions thousands of years ago happened because of humans, while some feel those extinctions occurred because of a changing global climate. Why the debate? Usually, it's because these people are so passionate about the environment that they want others to understand what they believe in order to help care for our planet.

If you're new to learning about the environment, the best advice is to listen to everyone's viewpoint, learn as much as you can, and figure out where you stand on the issues. This book will give you an overview of what's going on. The first half of the book explores the parts that make up the environment, and the second half touches on some of the issues that the environment currently faces. If a topic really interests you, head to the library to learn more or check out the list of resources in the back of the book. **Environmentalists** are usually eager to talk with others to share their knowledge.

About the Projects

In the first half of the book, you'll explore the different elements of the environment—land, water, air, sun, and life. Use the projects to enjoy how amazing our planet really is. It's so easy to forget. After all, you've lived here all your life and you may barely even notice the trees you pass every day on your way to school or that water you just slurped up from the water fountain. But all those parts are crucial to our existence. In the second half, you'll find projects that will help you take steps toward protecting the environment.

As you read and explore, be aware of the materials you use. For instance, you'll see many of the activities call for plastic, two-liter bottles. If you already get your drinks in this kind of bottle, it's a great way to recycle the container. If you don't get drinks in two-liter bottles, ask a neighbor or friend to save you one of theirs—that way, you're not making a purchase you don't need, and materials aren't being used to make an extra bottle that you wouldn't have purchased otherwise. Same with other materials used for activities. Ask at photo-processing centers for leftover film canisters or hardware stores for the scraps that are destined to be tossed out. See if you can buy items in bulk to reduce packaging, then divvy up the contents with a friend. Maybe you can come up with alternative materials for the projects so you can reuse something you already have. It's surprising the creative ways you can use things if you try to look at them differently.

Some of the projects involve living creatures or plants. Handle everything with great care, and return them, unharmed, to the place where you found them so they can continue playing their part in the environment. And (but you knew this already!) be sure to stay safe when you're working near a body of water or using a knife or tool.

Words to Know

environment: everything in nature—living or nonliving—including plants, animals, rocks, and water.

environmentalist: someone who works to preserve the environment.

Everyone Plays a Part

Most people do really care—people do love animals and nature. Few would think it's okay to pave over the national parks and chop down all the trees. People have humanity, people care about living things, and that's what you can tap into when you learn all you can about the environment—even parts of it that aren't cute and cuddly, like jaw-snapping crocodiles or freaky-looking spiders.

Although it can be easy to just sit back and say humans are responsible for all the woes in the environment, the fact is we're woven into the environment just as much as a leaf on a tree or the soil we walk on. If we had the power to mess things up a bit, we surely have the power to straighten things back out. As you learn about the environment, you'll find some people are extremely exuberant and even extreme in their ideas about taking care of the environment—just like there are other people who don't seem to care at all. Once you learn everything you can about how our environment works and some of the problems it's facing, you can figure out where you fit in. And learning about the environment and taking steps to protect it is really about doing your personal best—making choices that you can accept. If that means making some changes and not others, then some changes are better than none. If everyone tries, within their own limits, then some change is good.

There's no way to cover every environmental subject in depth in just one book, so use this book as a springboard to get started discovering the world around you. Pick out the parts that fascinate you, and have fun learning about the environment. Nature is full of amazing living and nonliving things—from incredible animal and plant adaptations to how the same water that you drink today may have been the water a dinosaur swam in. Get out and explore, and then come back and share your discoveries with everyone who will listen. Watching documentaries on television is a great way to learn—but getting out there and getting your hands on nature yourself is unbeatable.

Earth

Our Spot in Space

Imagine you're traveling across the Milky Way galaxy, closing in on a bright star. As you get closer, you realize it's our sun, and then you pass the planets with all the familiar names, getting closer and closer to home: Saturn, Jupiter, through the asteroid belt, Mars . . . all these are unique and interesting, but they're lacking something extra special: life. And then you see Earth.

Except for the few astronauts who were lucky enough to go into space, the rest of us didn't get our first glimpse of what Earth really looks

like until 1968. That's when Apollo 8 sent back what's now a famous photo of our planet—the familiar "blue marble," a gorgeous blue, brown, green, and white-swirled globe against the pitch darkness of space. Move in closer, and you whisk through the clouds toward your continent. When you're back with your feet on the ground, you see the plants, animals, and people that are familiar to you—your environment. Your home.

But what makes life on Earth possible? How can we live here and not, say, on the red planet of Mars? Why is the earth the only spot where life exists?

It's all about our star, the sun, and the way our planet is perfectly placed in the solar system. Our global **ecosystem** all starts with the sun, which provides the light, energy, and heat for living things on Earth to exist. It also activates our world's **water cycle**, evaporating water from lakes, oceans, and rivers. The water then condenses and falls again to Earth as rain, providing water to plant life. Plants are the source for all the global food chains—for humans and all the animals.

Our earth looks like a pretty rugged place. Add in the power we can see in nature, such as hurricanes, earthquakes, and molten lava, and it seems like nothing could hurt our strong planet. But, if you look closer, you'll find it's a world that needs to maintain a careful balance in order to continue to grow and flourish.

Anywhere you look in the world, the environment is playing a balancing act between plants, animals, and natural resources, such as fossil fuels and water. Take the **food chains**, for example. The sun provides energy to plants, which small animals—like rabbits and mice—eat. Then larger **carnivores** eat the smaller animals. Seems simple, right? But what if part of that food chain were to be disrupted?

That's what happened long ago with sea otters. From the late 1700s into the early 1900s, people relentlessly hunted sea otters for their fur. As the sea otter population declined, the sea urchins—the sea otters' favorite food—didn't have any predators gobbling them up. So the sea urchin population grew and gobbled up all the kelp (their favorite food). With less kelp in the sea, other animals like fish and small crabs disappeared because they needed the kelp beds as protective hiding places or for food sources. An entire mini-ecosystem was wiped out, all because the sea otters weren't around to keep the sea urchin population in balance.

Words to Know

ecosystem: a community interacting with its environment, creating a working system.

community: all the living things within a particular region that interact with each other.

water cycle: the process where the planet's water evaporates, condenses, and returns to Earth.

food chain: the feeding relationship between plants and animals in an environment.

carnivore: a creature that eats other creatures, also called a predator.

This example shows just how delicate the earth's systems really are. Food chains like this exist in every ecosystem. You can read more about food chains in chapter 5. This balance of our world, our environment, is so critical to life on the planet that we need to understand how it all works. Think about it: What happens to kids in the playground if they're on the seesaw and the other rider suddenly gets off? The balance is lost and it's a fast ride down. It's the same with our planet. If you change the balance, or break up any of the systems that are in place, it'll throw off the rest of the system.

Know Your Biome

Desert. One fifth of the earth's surface is made up of deserts. Talk about extremes. The desert is one extreme **habitat**. With very little rainfall and temperatures that can soar well over 120 degrees Fahrenheit, plants and animals that call the desert home are sparse. But they are there. And they are specially built to withstand high temperatures and dry conditions. Cactus and other plants have shallow roots to absorb any rain quickly. Desert dwellers, such as scorpions and kangaroo rats, are adapted to live on a minimal amount of water.

Tundra. Opposite the desert's heat is the chill of the tundra biome, which is the coldest biome on our planet. Temperatures can drop to 50 degrees or more below zero. Although it seems just too cold for animals, the tundra is actually home to quite a number of animals—among them caribou, seals, walrus, lemmings, and arctic hares—and the biggest predator of the tundra, the polar bear. There's less diversity in the plant life; only lichens, mosses, and some shrubs grow here.

Aquatic. The largest biome in the world, this includes all the water environments, from freshwater lakes to saltwater oceans. The marine biome covers about 70 percent of the earth's surface. The plants and animals living in an aquatic environment are diverse and plentiful, from the huge blue whale to the tiny plankton it eats.

Did You Know?

There's not a lot of agreement on how many biomes there are. Some scientists divide the world into 5, others 12, and some even believe there are over 100 "eco-regions."

8

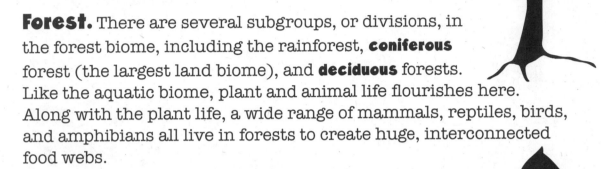

Forest. There are several subgroups, or divisions, in the forest biome, including the rainforest, **coniferous** forest (the largest land biome), and **deciduous** forests. Like the aquatic biome, plant and animal life flourishes here. Along with the plant life, a wide range of mammals, reptiles, birds, and amphibians all live in forests to create huge, interconnected food webs.

Grassland. Not surprisingly, grasses rule in the grasslands. The land is covered with different kinds of grasses that grow tall and in abundance, with hardly any trees or shrubs in sight. Animals that live here are mostly **herbivores**. Some examples of herbivores are: antelope, wild horses, or prairie dogs. But there are carnivores here too, such as lions.

Words to Know

biome: a large area inhabited by certain plants and animals that are well-adapted to the climate, geology, and water resources in the region.

habitat: a plant or animal's natural "home," where they can find the food, shelter, and other conditions that are best suited to meet their needs.

coniferous: plants and trees that do not shed their leaves each year.

deciduous: plants and trees that shed their leaves each year.

herbivore: a creature that eats plant material.

temperate: areas of land that fall between the polar regions and the tropics, with different climates and biomes.

subtropical: areas close to the tropics with weather that's usually very mild.

savannah: an area with wide open, grassy areas and scattered trees.

ecology: the interaction between organisms and their environment.

Biomes

What's really amazing about Earth is that geographic regions are so different from each other. Animals, plants, and weather conditions are different all around the globe. A polar bear that thrives in the Arctic wouldn't last long in the hot Sahara. And that sidewinder from the desert couldn't survive in the frozen tundra. Each different climate hosts diverse plants and animals that create their own balance within their biome.

The climate can be dramatically different within a relatively small area, too. Along the southwest coast of South America is a deciduous area where plants shed their leaves each year. Continuing east you'll hit a mountainous region, followed by a **temperate** grassland, then a desert zone.

The animals and vegetation that grow in any region are not only dependent upon each other, but the people of the region also depend on them for food. A meal of broiled fish may be standard fare for someone living in Japan near the ocean, while over in grassy South Africa, a maize-based porridge may be a favorite food.

Biomes aren't permanent, either. Take the Sahara Desert. Today it's about four million square miles of dry desert with an average of three inches of annual rainfall in the **subtropical** region. But 10,000 years ago, the Sahara wasn't a desert at all. It was a fertile **savannah** where elephants, giraffes, and other animals roamed, and plant life was abundant. Closer to the present time, human intervention transformed a biome. The Great Black Swamp was a wetland in northwest Ohio in the United States with vegetation like ash, elm, and maple trees. In the late nineteenth century, though, the swamp was drained, and today it's farmland.

Did You Know?

Penguins don't just live in the frozen Antarctic biome. They also live along the coast of South America, the Galapagos Islands, the southern coast of Africa, and along the coast of Australia.

Biome facts

Lake Baikal **in central Asia is the largest freshwater lake in the world—containing one fifth of the world's fresh water.**

✳

The Sahara Desert, **at about four million square miles, is the largest desert in the world. The entire continental United States could fit inside it.**

✳

The rainforests **offer Earth a living bounty. Over half of the world's insect, plant, and animal species live in the rainforests. In the rainforests of Costa Rica alone, for example, there are over 1,300 species of butterflies.**

✳

The real "final frontier" could be the ocean. **Scientists believe the Mariana Trench (in the western Pacific Ocean) is the deepest spot in the world at about seven miles. That's deeper than Mount Everest is high!**

Make Your Own
Whole World

1 Mix the dry ingredients, except for the brown sugar, together in the large baking dish. Mix in two cups of whole world add-ins—except for chocolate chips, pineapple, or raisins, if you're using them. These can be added after baking, so they don't melt or get too hard.

2 In the saucepan, mix together the honey, brown sugar, and oil. Heat over medium heat until the sugar dissolves, stirring constantly to make sure it doesn't burn.

3 Pour sugar mixture over the oat mixture and combine well. Be sure to coat as much of the dry mix as possible. Bake at 375 degrees Fahrenheit for 10 minutes, or until it's crunchy enough for your taste.

4 Let the granola cool in the pan before breaking it into chunks and mixing in the rest of the add-ins (the chocolate chips, dried pineapple, and raisins). Store in an airtight container.

Supplies

large baking dish
1/2 cup dry milk
5 cups dry oatmeal
1 teaspoon cinnamon
pinch of salt
whole world "add ins"
small saucepan
1/3 cup honey
3/4 cup brown sugar
1/3 cup vegetable oil
airtight container

Granola

Whole-World Add-Ins

Because of the different habitats around the world, different plants flourish in some places naturally. You can sample foods from around the world when you stir two cups (total) of any of these international ingredients into your granola to make it a truly whole-world product.

Cinnamon is the dried bark of a type of evergreen tree. Indonesia is one of the largest producers of cinnamon.

Chocolate comes from the seed of the tropical cacao tree. Most of the world's supply comes from the eastern coast of Africa.

Raisins are a product of the United States, and the result of drying grapes.

Coconut is the (really big!) seed from the coconut palm tree. Coconut comes from the Philippines and Indonesia. Use coconut shavings for your granola recipe.

Brazil nuts are the seeds from a Brazil nut fruit, and they grow in South America. They're considered an important non-timber product of the rainforests.

Pineapple is a familiar fruit that grows in Hawaii. Use dried pineapple for your granola recipe.

Dates are the fruit of the date palm tree, which grows in the Middle East.

Almonds come from a tree native to Asia.

Sunflower seeds are the seeds from the cheerful sunflower, native to the Americas.

Sesame seeds are the somewhat oily seeds from the sesame plant, which grows in tropical regions.

Pecans, from the southern region of the United States, are similar to walnuts.

Dried cranberries come from cranberry trees growing in cool, boggy areas.

Maple syrup is made from the sap of maple trees in northeastern North America.

Make Your Own
Tullgren Funnel

The earth you walk on is more complex than you may realize—not only is the geology fascinating, but the ground is also home to animals you probably don't even know are there. Scientists who want to study the very small creatures who live in the soil and leaf litter use a Berlese-Tullgren Funnel, named after the scientists who created it over one hundred years ago. You can uncover some of these incredible little critters when you create a funnel yourself.

1 Wrap the black construction paper around the jar so it covers the outside. Secure it with tape.

2 Cut a small piece of mesh (an old screen is ideal) and place it in the bottom of the funnel so it blocks the hole. Set the funnel into the mouth of the jar. This will prevent your soil or leaf litter from falling into your collection.

3 Fill the funnel with fresh soil. If you're using leaf litter, it may work best if you get the leaf litter that's at the very bottom of the pile you find. Or, try setting up a couple of different systems using soil in one and leaf litter from different layers or from different locations in another.

Supplies

black construction paper
large jar
tape
scissors
small piece of mesh or strainer
funnel
soil or leaf litter
desk lamp
magnifying glass or microscope

Words to Know

leaf litter: fallen leaves and other dead plant material that is starting to break down.

4 Set up the desk lamp so that it shines down directly on the soil or leaf litter in the funnel, but not so close that it burns it.

5 Wait about an hour. As the tiny creatures in the soil or leaf litter try to move away from the light and heat, they'll move downward through the funnel and fall into your jar.

Did You Know?

There may be as many as 10 million species of insects on Earth.

6 After the time is up, take the construction paper off your jar and examine the critters you've found using your magnifying glass or microscope. You may find critters like mites, nematods (microscopic worms), and earthworms and beetles. The larger creatures will be at the screen in the bottom of the funnel, since they won't fit through. These creatures are important to the ecosystem because they are often the beginning of food chains. As plants and animals decay, these critters consume the organic matter directly or the bacteria and fungi that break down plant and animal matter. Then, they're eaten by larger creatures who live in the soil, who are then consumed by larger insects or birds.

7 After you've examined what you've found, be sure to release everything back to the soil.

Air,
All Around Us

Air surrounds us here on Earth. You can't see it or smell it—although you can see pollutants like smoke in the air. But Earth's **atmosphere**, the mixture of gases that blanket the globe, is a vital part of our environment, because it's critical to life on our planet.

Not only does the atmosphere supply the **oxygen** that we need to breathe, but it also protects us from the sun's **ultraviolet** rays. And it also acts like insulation—soaking up most of the sun's incredible heat so the temperatures on the surface of Earth can sustain life. What's more, the lowest level of the atmosphere is where our weather occurs, part of the water cycle that brings us necessary rain.

But what is air really? Do you think it's oxygen? You're partly right. Air is made up of a mixture of gases, and oxygen is one of them.

Did You Know?

Plants actually "breathe" out carbon dioxide, just like we do. But they also produce oxygen after photosynthesis, which is one reason they're so important to the environment.

It's also made of nitrogen and small amounts of **carbon dioxide**, a gas called argon, and some other trace gases. Pretty much all living **organisms** need oxygen to survive on Earth. The few organisms that don't need oxygen are called anaerobic and live in oxygen-free places like the hot volcano vents in the ocean.

The plants that surround you—trees, houseplants, grass, bushes—all "breathe" air just as living creatures do. Instead of lungs, though, plants use microscopic openings on their leaves to take in gases and release moisture and oxygen. These tiny openings are called stomata. A plant can even close the stomata to retain moisture at night or if conditions are too dry. Plants take in the carbon dioxide in the air through the stomata. Using chlorophyll, the green substance in their leaves, plants use the carbon dioxide to make glucose, which provides energy the plant needs to live. When sunlight reaches the plant's leaves, it starts the **photosynthesis** process, and the oxygen molecules that are left over from the glucose-making process are released into the air.

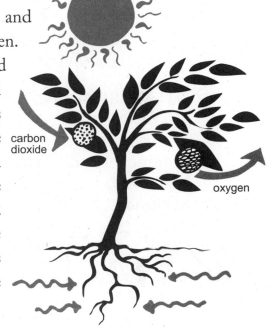

carbon dioxide

oxygen

Fish Need Air, Too

Fish, surrounded by water, need air to breathe, too. Oxygen is dissolved in water, and fish get the oxygen they need through their gills. A fish opens its mouth and takes in water. When the fish closes its mouth, the water passes over its gills, which contain filaments and capillaries that can extract the oxygen from the water—up to 85 percent of the available oxygen—and send it into the fish's bloodstream.

Up Into the Stratosphere . . .
Wherever **That** Is

Earth's atmosphere is in layers:

Troposphere. This is the layer that's at our level—starting from the ground up. It reaches up about 12 miles, thicker at some parts of the globe than others. Airplanes fly in this layer of the atmosphere, and it's where most of Earth's weather happens, too. The higher up you go, the colder it gets.

Stratosphere. This layer rises up from the troposphere to a height of around 30 miles. Unlike the troposphere, it gets hotter in the stratosphere the higher up you go. There's no weather here and commercial airplanes can't fly this high, but weather balloons do go up into the stratosphere. Ozone, which is gas created by ultraviolet **radiation** from the sun interacting with oxygen, is in the stratosphere, helping protect Earth from harmful ultraviolet radiation.

Did You Know?

People sometimes think air is mostly oxygen—but it's not. Most of the air we breathe, 78 percent, is actually nitrogen, and only 21 percent is oxygen.

Mesosphere. The mesosphere rises up about 56 miles above Earth's surface. Together with the stratosphere, it's considered the "middle atmosphere." Many **meteors** burn up when they enter the mesosphere. We see them as shooting stars.

Thermosphere. The thickest part of the atmosphere, the thermosphere rises up over 300 miles above the surface of Earth. The space shuttle orbits in the thermosphere.

Exosphere. The last layer of the atmosphere, the exosphere is where any gases begin to thin and the molecules separate and drift into space.

Ozone—What's the Buzz About?

Ozone gets a lot of attention, usually in a negative way. But the ozone is actually helpful. At least, when it's where it belongs, which is up in the stratosphere. There's even a saying: "Ozone: Good up high, bad nearby." Ozone is a gas made up of three oxygen atoms (we breathe oxygen made up of two oxygen atoms). It forms a kind of shield against the sun's harmful ultraviolet (UV) rays. But when harmful gases from things such as some aerosol cans or air conditioners rise up to the ozone, they make the ozone weaker so it can't do its job as well.

Then there's tropospheric ozone, down here at our level. It's man-made—caused by pollution from things like car exhaust. That's when it's not good, because when we inhale ozone, it's bad for our lungs. Ozone usually forms when it's hot—in the summer on hot afternoons. And although it's usually in heavily populated areas in urban and suburban settings, the winds can carry it far into rural areas, too.

Words to Know

atmosphere: all of the air surrounding a planet.

oxygen: the most abundant element on Earth, found in the air and in the water.

ultraviolet: invisible radiation produced by the sun.

carbon dioxide: CO_2, a heavy colorless gas with molecules containing one carbon atom and two oxygen atoms. It is formed mostly by the combustion and decomposition of organic substances— such as when animals breathe and when animal and vegetable matter decays.

decompose: separate back down into its parts or elements.

persist: endure or not break down at all, even over time.

organism: something living, such as a plant or an animal.

photosynthesis: the process in which plants use sunlight, water, and carbon dioxide to create energy.

radiation: very fast heat transfer.

meteor: a streak of light produced when a small particle from outer space enters the earth's atmosphere.

Blowing in the Wind

So we can't usually see air—but we can see the work air does when it's moving, whether it's gently rustling the leaves on the trees or whipping up desert sands into an intense sandstorm. Winds are the result of both moving air masses in the lower levels of the atmosphere and the rotation of Earth.

Did You Know?

Spanish fishermen noticed the warmer waters arriving around Christmas time, and named them "El Niño." This means "the little boy" in Spanish, and refers to the birth of Christ.

When the sun shines down on Earth, land masses absorb the heat while the water areas reflect most of it back, warming the air. As the air warms, it gets lighter and rises. If there's any cool air mass nearby (perhaps over land), it will rush in to fill that space because it's denser and heavier. When the air moves, it creates wind.

Wind doesn't always blow in one direction, either. Along the coast, the wind blows from sea to shore, as the land heats up quickly during the day. But, at night, the water retains heat longer than land, so the winds change direction and blow from the land to sea.

While winds can change according to different weather patterns, there are some that are predictable depending on the seasons of the year. People in southern California are familiar with the hot **Santa Ana winds** that stir up in late summer, for example.

There are also wind patterns that form around the **equator** that blow from east to west. The winds blow west to east in the **mid-latitudes**, and east to west again near the poles. These winds are called **trade winds**, because back in the times of sailing merchant ships, they helped move the ships across the ocean, and they defined the routes that the ships went.

As the trade winds blow across the surface of the water, they set the water in motion, creating currents that affect the climates around the globe. There are some years, however, that the trade winds don't blow. It happens anywhere from two to ten years apart. It's called **El Niño**, and it has an impact on the entire earth. What happens is this: When the winds from South America stop, cool water is no longer pushed west, and the water warms up. The water warms up all the way up the west coast of the Americas, even as far as Washington state. The result? Air masses all over the globe are affected, and abnormal weather patterns result.

Wind Power

The force of the wind can be catastrophic in some cases—just think of a hurricane. But, it can also be harnessed to create a clean energy source, like sailboats use. Our ancestors used boats with sails to travel to new lands to explore. And around the seventh century, people began using windmills to grind grain between millstones.

Using a **turbine**, wind power can be converted to energy like electricity. As people continue looking for better ways to produce energy, wind power use continues to climb every year. Denmark is the world leader in wind power; 20 percent of electricity in Denmark is generated by the wind.

Words to Know

Santa Ana winds: winds that occur in Southern California when air changes temperature moving over mountains.

equator: an invisible circle around the earth midway between the North and South Poles.

mid-latitudes: the areas between the equator and the North and South Poles.

trade winds: winds that blow almost continually toward the equator from the northeast north of the equator and from the southeast south of the equator.

El Niño: unusually warm ocean conditions occurring every few years along the tropical west coast of South America, which have dramatic effects on weather patterns around the world.

turbine: a rotary engine, usually using a blade, that converts one type of energy to another, such as wind energy into electricity.

Make Your Own
Wind-Powered

The wind created by a fan will not only generate the power to turn this bubble machine on, but also blow the bubbles, too.

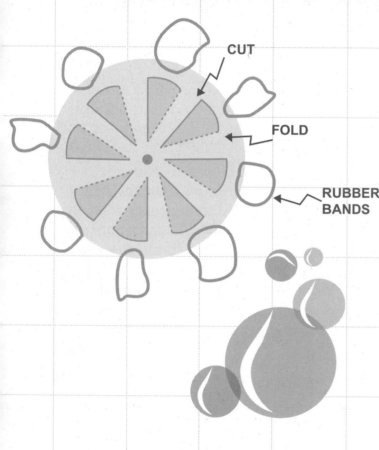

CUT

FOLD

RUBBER
BANDS

1 Cut eight flaps around the lid and bend the flaps back so they stand up. Don't cut all the way to the center. Leave about an inch and a half circle uncut. The flaps will catch the wind to power your bubble machine.

2 Using the hot glue, carefully glue the small rubber bands around the outside of the lid, spacing them evenly. These will be the "dippers" that go into the bubble solution, so glue only one end of the rubber bands to the circle and leave most of the rubber band flopping free (see diagram). They don't need to be perfect circles.

Did You Know?

Some plants depend on the wind to spread their seeds. The sycamore tree, with its helicopter-shaped seeds, needs the wind to carry the wing-shaped seeds to new ground where they can sprout. Even dandelions, with their familiar puffed seeds, need the wind to scatter them all over your yard.

Bubble Machine

Supplies

plastic lid (a coffee can lid is perfect)

scissors

hot glue gun and glue sticks

small rubber bands

small nail

ink pen

bubble solution

bowl or shallow pan

rubber bands, packing tape or bungee cords

cardboard box

large fan

Did You Know?

The strongest "regular" surface wind ever recorded was 231 miles per hour at the top of Mount Washington in New Hampshire. Tornados have been known to blow even stronger.

3 Using a small nail, poke a hole in the center of the lid. Then, take the pen and carefully pull the ink tube out from its plastic case. This will be your axle. Push the ink part of the pen through the hole you made in the lid. You'll want to be sure it's nice and snug in the little hole you made. The pen should stop when it gets to the tip. Then, slide the pen case back onto the ink tube. When you hold the pen case, you should be able to spin your lid freely.

4 You're now ready to assemble your machine. In front of the fan, place a shallow pan filled with the bubble solution. Then, mount your bubble machine by using rubber bands, packing tape or bungees to hold the pen case down firmly on top of a cardboard box or stack of books. It's important that the rubber bands on the lid be completely submerged in the bubble solution, without dragging on the bottom. Experiment until you find the perfect height. Turn the fan on and watch the power of wind at work!

Make Your Own
Plant-Oxygen Experiment

This experiment will help you see that plants really do "breathe." Even though they don't have lungs, plants do releases gas into the air—just like we do.

1 Take one of the plant's runners and carefully insert it into the bottom of the test tube or drinking glass. Try to find a runner that's small enough that it doesn't touch the end of the test tube or the top of the glass.

2 Put two or three lumps of modeling clay around the rim of the test tube. This will help it stick in the bottom of the bowl when you invert it.

3 Fill the large bowl with water, and fill the test tube with water to the very top.

4 Carefully flip the test tube over so that no water escapes and submerge it into the bowl of water. Stick it to the bottom of the bowl using the modeling clay. If you're having trouble keeping water in the test tube when you flip it, try holding a plastic card (like an old credit card) tightly over the top of the tube, then flipping it and sliding the card off once the tube is underwater.

5 Set the plant and the bowl with the test tube in direct sunlight and wait a couple of hours. When you return, you'll see a pocket of gas at the top of the tube where the plant has released oxygen and forced the water out from the tube. The plant leaf has released oxygen after its photosynthesis and displaced the water from the tube. If you wait longer, you can see how the plant produces more oxygen, which it normally releases into the environment, unseen.

Supplies

plant with runners such as a spider plant

test tube or clear narrow drinking glass

modeling clay

large bowl

Make Your Own
Giant Air Blaster

Feel how strong air can be when you make this giant air blaster. Stack up some paper cups, aim your blaster carefully, and give the stretched plastic a whack to send them flying.

1 Using the wire snips, cut a two-inch hole in the middle of the bottom of the bucket. You might want to get an adult to help you with this.

2 Stretch the plastic tightly over the top of the bucket, and secure it with the bungee cord.

3 To fire your blaster, hold it sideways with the hole pointing at whatever you want to blast. Sharply rap the plastic with your fist or a stick. The movement of the air in the bucket, forced quickly through the smaller hole, will create a rushing gust of "wind."

Did You Know?

Turbines only need an average wind speed of 14 miles per hour to convert wind energy to electricity.

Supplies

heavy-duty wire snips

one 15-gallon bucket

large plastic sheet (an old shower curtain will work)

bungee cord

paper cups

Water, Water
Everywhere

Water is essential to all life on Earth. Without it, you wouldn't be reading this book. Your body needs water. In fact, your brain alone is about 70 percent water. Your cells, and the cells of every living thing, need water to function and survive.

Fortunately, water makes up almost 71 percent of the entire Earth. It's primarily saltwater; less than 3 percent of Earth's water is freshwater. And, here's something really interesting: The water that's on Earth today, in all forms—salt water, freshwater, rain, ponds, even a kids' tears—

is the same water that's been around since Earth was formed. It can be frozen in the tundra, stored inside a cactus in the desert, or guzzled down after a soccer game, but it always finds its way back into the water cycle eventually, to be used for something else for another million years. That sip of water you just took could have also quenched a T-rex's thirst millions of years ago.

So what is the water cycle? It's a never-ending process in which water makes a loop through the environment. Water falls from the clouds as **precipitation**, which can take different forms, such as rain, snow, or sleet. Most of this falls into the oceans (because the surface area of Earth's oceans is almost 140 million square miles, it's hard to miss!). It could be absorbed into the ground or run off rocks or pavement into streams and rivers. Animals use the water that falls or runs off into streams and rivers as their habitat or as drinking water as it flows back toward the ocean.

If water falls on land where there are plenty of plants, the plants use the water—and they need a lot of it to grow and photosynthesize. Water that's not used by plants gets absorbed into the soil and travels through a filtering process through layers of permeable rock, such as sandstone, to a "holding tank" deep underground called the water table. The water flows through the water table slowly, eventually returning to the ocean.

Words to Know

precipitation: falling moisture resulting from condensation in the water cycle, in the form of rain, sleet, snow, etc.

evaporate: to convert from liquid to vapor.

vapor: suspended in the air as a gas, like steam, mist, or fog.

condense: to convert from vapor to liquid.

The heat of the sun warms the water in lakes and oceans. As the water gets warmer, the surface water starts **evaporating** and becomes water **vapor**. It rises into cooler air, where it **condenses** and eventually returns to Earth as precipitation. Then the cycle begins again.

Ocean Currents

Just as there are different wind patterns that blow with relative consistency around the globe, there are also regular ocean currents that draw different temperatures of water around Earth. Warm currents, water that flows from warmer areas (the equator), bring higher temperatures and more precipitation to an area. The reverse is true of colder currents. Strong winds blowing across the surface of the ocean have an impact on the currents, steering them in their direction. The rotation of Earth also is responsible for currents.

Well-known currents include the Gulf Stream, which starts in the Gulf of Mexico and flows past Florida and the eastern United States before heading over across the Atlantic Ocean where it splits in two. Half of the current travels up to northern Europe and the other half swings back down the coast of Africa. The Gulf Stream helps keep Florida's winter air temperatures warm.

The strongest ocean current is the Antarctic Circumpolar Current, which flows from west to east around the continent of Antarctica. It connects the Indian, Pacific, and Atlantic ocean basins. Since there are no land masses in the way, the current flows all the way around the world with nothing to slow it down or weaken it.

From **Puddles** To **Oceans**

Do you know all the different bodies of water that cover the earth?

ocean: these are the five major bodies of salt water—Arctic, Antarctic (also called the Southern Ocean), Atlantic, Indian, and Pacific.

lake: a very large body of water, usually freshwater. Lakes are important to the environment because they support a wide range of ecosystems, supplying water and habitat to a variety of animals and plants.

sea: a large body of water that is salty, not fresh, water.

river: a large, moving body of water that travels from higher to lower **elevation**.

stream: a small, moving body of water that usually feeds into a river.

Words to Know

elevation: how high something is above sea level.

glacier: an enormous mass of ice and snow that moves slowly with the pull of gravity.

thermal vents: grooves in the earth's surface emitting very hot water heated from deep within the earth.

salinity: the amount of salt in water or another liquid.

buoyant: light and floating.

Glaciers

About 75 percent of Earth's freshwater is trapped in **glaciers**, mostly in Greenland and Antarctica, but also in places like Alaska and on very high mountain peaks. If all the glaciers were to melt, the ocean levels would rise over 200 feet. Glaciers are constantly moving—advancing and retreating as the ice melts and then freezes again. They grind huge, smooth, U-shaped valleys in the earth as they ponderously scrape over the ground, like a frozen river flowing. Even after the glacier has long gone, the changes on the landscape still remain in the form of valleys and hills. Although glaciers usually move slowly—some move about four inches a day—sometimes a glacier "surges," moving anywhere between 10 to 100 times faster than its usual rate. Scientists are keeping an eye on the retreating glaciers as an indicator of our global climate health. Many believe that global warming is causing the glaciers to melt at a much faster speed than in the past.

Did You Know?

Salt water is denser than freshwater—that's why it's easier to swim in the ocean than in a freshwater lake. The salt helps keep your body **buoyant**.

Salt in the Ocean

Even if you've never tasted ocean water, you know that it's salty. The salt in the ocean comes from land. Salt (sodium chloride) is a mineral that occurs naturally in rocks—it's the same stuff that's on your kitchen table, too. Over millions of years, as rain, rivers, and streams ran over the rocks, they washed some sodium chloride into the water. Since the water cycle flows through the ocean before evaporation, the salt is left behind in the ocean. Underwater volcanoes and **thermal vents** also add to the **salinity**. The salt has built up over millions of years to its present salty content.

Make Your Own
Water-Testing Experiment

Every liquid, including water, has an acidity level, which is its chemical composition. How acidic something is determines how it will interact with other compounds. Distilled water is an exception. It has a neutral pH, which means it's neither acidic nor alkaline. You can rank liquids on a scale from the most acidic to the most alkaline, using pH test paper to determine a liquid's acidity. You'll learn more about acidity on page 65.

1 First you need to create a chart to use when you compare your water samples (see "Charting Your Samples"). Collect samples from different sources: a pond, bottled water, rainwater, a street puddle, your tap water, etc.

2 First, test the pH of each sample to see what the acidity is (check your chart for comparison).

3 Run each sample through a coffee filter into a catch container. If you want, run the water through another clean filter again to see if there's more sediment. If you have a microscope, or even a magnifying glass, take a peek at what was in the water.

Supplies

piece of paper

samples to test for pH (see list)

pH test paper (at aquarium stores, pet stores, or drugstores)

water collecting containers (empty film canisters work well)

coffee filters

Charting Your Samples

Use your imagination to find a lot of different samples to fill your comparison chart. For each, dip a pH paper into them and find their acidity. Acids turn pH paper red; compare the shade of color on your paper with the indicator that came with the package of pH paper. Then, list the liquids in order on your paper, making note of the pH number for each liquid. Some other liquids to try:

- distilled water
- dissolved baking soda
- vinegar
- ammonia
- milk
- lemon juice

Make Your Own
Backyard Pond

Even if you've only got a very small backyard, you can still create a pond to enjoy—just dig a smaller hole. If you only have patio or deck space, you can create an above-ground pond by using a watertight container.

1 Find a good location for your pond. Consider whether your plants need full or partial sunlight, or if overhanging trees will drop too many leaves into the pond during the autumn.

2 Dig the space out for your pond. If you'll have critters living in your pond (e.g. frogs or turtles), you may want to dig it out so there are two levels—a shallow rim around your pond, perhaps a foot or so deep, and a deeper level in the middle that is a couple of feet deep so your aquatic life will have a place to swim down to in order to escape predators. Be sure you're not digging an area that's larger than your plastic sheet.

3 Spread the plastic sheet over the area you've dug, making sure it spreads all the way up the sides. Try to bring the sheet over the edges of your pond. Don't worry how it looks. You can cover it up with rocks and soil later.

4 Pour sand, rocks, or other bottom cover over your plastic sheet. This will weight it down and prevent the sheet from floating up. Cover up the plastic sheet around the edges of your pond with large rocks or soil and grass seed.

5 Fill your pond. If you're using water from the hose, wait at least a week for the chemicals to filter out of the water before adding any plants or critters.

6 Introduce the plants to your pond, setting some pots along the shallow edges and others, such as water lilies, deeper. Talk to your local plant nursery to learn about what kinds of plants are best for your area. Add water to your "pond" periodically as necessary to keep it full.

Supplies

shovel

thick plastic, such as a heavy shower curtain. Make sure it doesn't have holes!

sand and rocks

water plants in pots

a hose or water supply

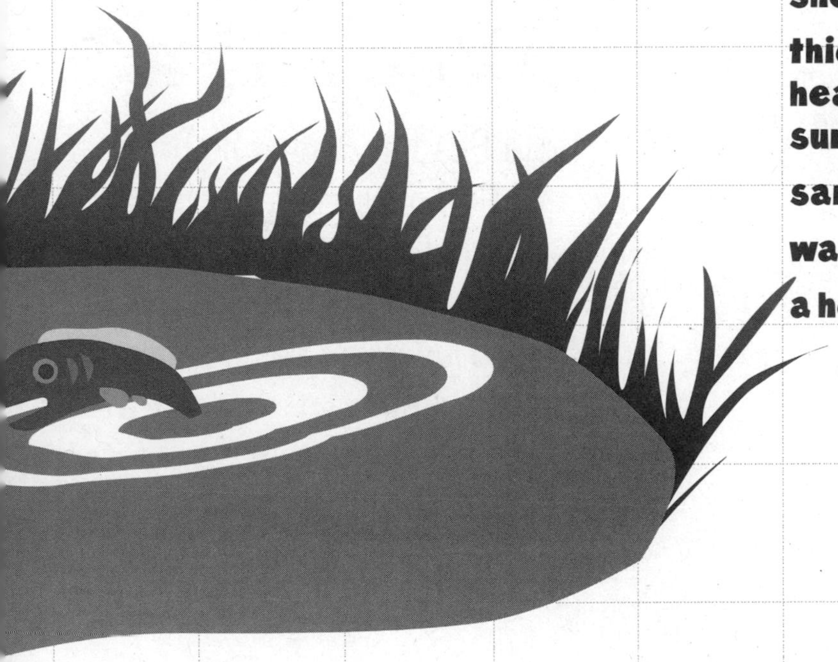

Make Your Own
Miniature Water Cycle

You can see the water cycle in action by using solar power to warm up a bowl of water. The water will evaporate, and the plastic wrap will catch the water vapor. As more water vapor gathers, it will condense and "rain" back into your bowl.

1 Fill the bowl with a couple inches of water. Stretch the plastic wrap over the top of the bowl and secure it around the opening with rubber bands. Set the stone in the middle of the wrap. Place the bowl in direct sunlight.

2 Before long, you'll see water droplets collecting on the plastic wrap as the evaporating water condenses back into liquid form. The stone you put on top will make a low point for the water to collect on when it condenses. If you wait, the droplets will become so heavy they'll "rain" back down into the bowl.

3 Try it again with salt water. You can get it right from the ocean if you're near a beach, or just mix in table salt. The "rain" that falls will not be salty. It will be fresh water because the salt stays behind. Take some of the salt water and put it on a plate outside, in direct sunlight. When the water evaporates, you'll see the salt that remains.

Did You Know?

The Dead Sea has such a high concentration of salt that it's over eight times saltier than the ocean. It's so salty because it's land-locked (no rivers or streams flow from it) and it's at a very low elevation. The water can't go anywhere except through evaporation—leaving all that salt behind. It's so dense you can't really swim in the Dead Sea. You just bob like a cork.

Supplies

clear bowl

water

plastic wrap

rubber bands

small stone

table salt (optional)

Make Your Own
Terrarium

Let the water cycle work to create a beautiful plantscape for your home. By trapping the water vapor inside your terrarium, it will keep your plants moist when it condenses again and trickles down the sides to the soil.

1 Cut the soda bottle's neck and top curve off so you have a straight cylinder with a domed bottom. If your bottle has the black cap on the bottom, remove it by wiggling a table knife around the base and twisting it gently. You can use this bottom instead of the small plastic container. You'll need the plastic container if your bottle didn't have a black bottom.

2 Fill the plastic container or black bottom with soil. Plant two or three seeds, or if you're using plants, plant one or two plants. Good plants for terrariums are slow-growing plants, such as miniature African violets or ferns. Gently moisten the soil.

3 Slide the upside-down soda bottle over the top of your base and secure it with wide tape if it's loose.

4 Set the terrarium in a well-lit place (but not in direct light). Soon you'll see the water cycle in action as water in the air within the terrarium collects on the sides and slides down to water the soil and your plant.

Supplies

one plastic two-liter soda bottle

small plastic container, such as a margarine tub

soil

seeds or small plants

water

wide tape

Our Star, The Sun

Every morning you can count on it: In virtually every location around the globe, the sun rises in the east. And it sets every evening in the west. It's one of Earth's most reliable and familiar rhythms, and it has been since Earth was formed.

For thousands of years, people have worshipped the sun as it followed its familiar path across the sky, bringing life and light to Earth. Farmers depend on it for their crops. Plants need it for photosynthesis. And for some, sunrises and sunsets are the stuff of songs and poems.

Our star, the sun, is the largest celestial body in our solar system. About a million Earths would fit inside the sun. And it's the only resident in our solar system that can produce its own energy. But scientists say in comparison to other stars in the universe, the sun isn't really that big.

It's called a **yellow dwarf** and is about one-sixth the size of a giant star. But, it's plenty hot for life on Earth. Even though the earth is about 93 million miles away from the sun, there are places on the earth where the temperature rises to over 150 degrees from the sun's rays. And think about this: Earth is only receiving two billionths of the sun's rays!

Unlike Earth, which is solid, the sun is a mass of gases. About 75 percent of the sun is composed of an **element** called **hydrogen**, and about 25 percent of the sun is the element **helium**. The sun generates its heat and light through an explosive process called **nuclear fusion**. Nuclear fusion is when hydrogen fuses into helium, producing energy and light and converting four million tons of matter into energy every second. In just over eight seconds, the sun's light reaches Earth.

Living Creatures and The Sun

Plants depend on the sun for photosynthesis. The sun's rays give the chlorophyll inside the plant's cells the energy needed to convert water and carbon dioxide to **glucose**. Plants need glucose for energy, and when they make glucose they also make oxygen, which is given off as a by-product. The energy stored inside the plant's cells gets transferred to animals when they consume the plants. Living creatures use this energy to grow, build and repair cells, and perform other necessary life functions.

Ectothermic reptiles need the sun to warm their bodies so they can digest food and have energy to move around. And humans need the sun for our bodies to make **vitamin D**.

Words to Know

yellow dwarf: a small star, such as our own sun.

element: a simple substance that is made up of only one kind of atom, such as oxygen.

hydrogen: the lightest and simplest element.

helium: a light element, usually found in gases, and often used to inflate balloons.

nuclear fusion: when hydrogen fuses into helium, producing energy and light.

glucose: the substance that makes up sugar crystals.

ectotherm: an organism–like a snake–whose body temperature is affected by the environment.

vitamin D: a vitamin that is important for bones and teeth. It is found in egg yolks and milk, and it can be produced in the body from sunlight.

Solar Power

The sun is the main energy producer on our planet. Not only in obvious ways, like the heating of the earth and water, but also in less direct or obvious ways. When the sun heats air masses they begin to move, which creates wind power. When the sun heats the oceans, water evaporates, enters the water cycle, and falls to Earth, feeding rivers and streams that can then generate energy.

The sun's energy from millions of years ago is helping us today, too, in the form of **fossil fuels**. Long ago, the energy passed from the sun to plants and animals, and stayed in the plants and animals throughout their lifetimes. After those living creatures died and fossilized, after millions (FC) of years, their remains became fossil fuels.

These fuels are limited though. When they're used up, they're gone for good. The good news is that **solar power** is renewable—it's constantly radiating down to Earth. Solar power can be used for heating businesses, homes, and pools. It can also generate electricity and even power solar cars.

Did You Know?

"The surface of the sun itself is 10,000 degrees Fahrenheit, but the core is a scorching 27 million degrees."

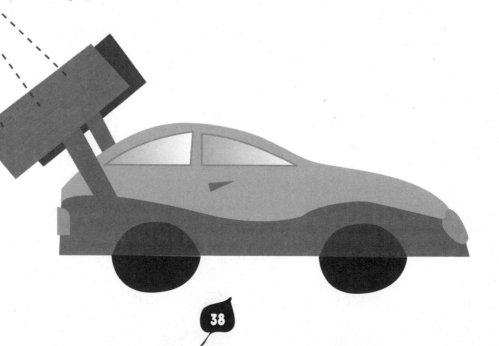

Telling Time and Location With the Sun

Although ancient people believed the sun revolved around the earth, we now understand it's the other way around. Early explorers knew Earth's rotation on its axis and revolving path around the sun could give them a pretty accurate way of knowing the time and their location.

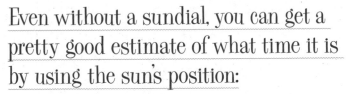

The earth is always in motion around the sun, turning on its axis and revolving in its orbit around the sun. Therefore, any shadows the sun casts upon the ground are going to change over the course of a day and throughout the year. Just poking a stick into the ground and examining its shadow can't give you an accurate time of day. The first **sundials** that were accurate used an angled piece of wood to account for the **curvature of the earth**. The shadow fell onto a chart that marked the hours of the day.

Even without a sundial, you can get a pretty good estimate of what time it is by using the sun's position:

- **Find the position of the sun.** And be careful, all those warnings your mom has given about not looking directly at the sun are true. Studies have found that your eyes can sustain damage from the sun, so be sure you never look at it directly.

- **If the sun is directly overhead,** you're in luck: It's noon. **If it's not noon** yet, determine which direction is east by finding the horizon that the sun is closest to. If it's past noon, the sun will be closer to the western horizon.

- **Divide the sky into four sections** that are about equal (the halfway point should pass directly over your head). Note which of those quadrants the sun is in.

Did You Know?

In the budding stages, the well-named sunflowers follow the sun's path during the day. In the morning, the flowers wake up facing the east, and turn their heads as the sun crosses the sky until they end in the evening facing the west. Older plants usually remain facing east.

- **Each of your quadrants represents** about a three-hour period. If the sun's in the first eastern quadrant, it's about between 6 a.m. and 9 a.m. If it's in the first western quadrant, it's between 3 p.m. and 6 p.m.
- **You can get closer still** by estimating how far along in the quadrant the sun is. For example, halfway through the far quadrant it will be about 7:30 a.m.

You can also tell direction using the sun. Here's how:

- **Push a stick** that's about three feet long into the ground. Pick an area that's relatively flat and free of debris so the stick will cast a good shadow on the ground.
- **Mark the spot** where the top of the stick's shadow falls. You can use a stone, twig, or whatever's handy. This spot will be your marker for west.
- **Wait about 15 minutes,** then mark the tip of the stick's shadow again (leave the original marker in place). This is your marker for east.
- **When you draw a line** connecting these two markers, you'll have a line that runs about east to west. If you position yourself with the east marker to your right and the west marker to the left, you'll be facing north, and south will be behind you.

Midnight Sun

In latitudes deep in the Arctic and Antarctic polar regions, there are times when the sunrise and sunset rhythm isn't the same as what you're familiar with. These parts of the globe are often called the "land of the midnight sun." When the earth is tilted toward the sun during the **summer solstice**, the sun shines for 24 hours straight in the **Arctic Circle**. And during the **winter solstice**, the sun shines a full day on the **Antarctic Circle**. Depending on how far north you are, the midnight sun can last for up to three months.

NORTH POLE

Ultraviolet Rays

The sun sends different wavelengths of energy to Earth. Although the ozone in the stratosphere blocks much of the harmful ultraviolet (UV) light, it doesn't absorb it all. In fact, there are three types of ultraviolet rays given off by the sun, and the ozone only absorbs one type, UVC, completely. Of the other two, the ozone absorbs UVB only partially and doesn't absorb UVA at all. These are the ultraviolet rays that can cause sunburn or even cancer.

UVB levels are at their strongest around noon, when the sun's rays are coming down directly on the surface of the earth. When the rays are at an angle to the earth, in the early morning and early evening, the UV levels aren't as strong.

Also, you may be more likely to get a sunburn when you're vacationing in the tropics—because the sun is positioned more directly overhead at the equator, and because the protective ozone is thinner over the tropics, the UV impact will be greater there.

Words to Know

fossil fuels: coal, oil, and natural gas.

solar power: energy from the sun converted to electricity.

sundial: a tool that uses a shadow cast by the sun to determine the time.

curvature of the earth: the way that the earth is shaped.

summer solstice: June 21 or 22, the day of the year when the Northern Hemisphere receives the most hours of daylight and the Southern Hemisphere receives the least.

Arctic Circle: the invisible ring around the northern part of the earth that begins at about 66 degrees north of the equator.

winter solstice: December 21 or 22, the day of the year when the Northern Hemisphere receives the fewest hours of daylight and the Southern Hemisphere receives the most.

Antarctic Circle: the invisible ring around the southern part of the earth that begins at about 66 degrees south of the equator.

Make Your Own...
Solar-Powered Oven

Can you harness solar energy to cook? With this solar-powered oven you can. It'll take a little time (so be patient!) but if you direct the sun's rays carefully onto your food, it will actually cook.

1 Trace a square on the lid of your pizza box. The square should be about an inch smaller than the lid.

2 Cut three sides of the square from the top of the pizza box. Leave the fourth side (the side along the back) uncut to form a flap.

3 Open the box and cover the window you just cut with plastic wrap. Try to tape it as tightly as possible so it's nice and taut.

4 Line the inside of the box, including the sides, with foil. Also line the inside of the flap you cut with foil.

5 Cover the inside bottom of the box with the black paper, fabric, or paint. This will help absorb the sun's heat.

Supplies

pizza box

scissors

plastic wrap (the thicker, the better)

tape (don't use duct tape—it releases toxic fumes)

aluminum foil

black construction paper, black fabric, or black paint

ruler or other object to prop open the top

oven thermometer (optional)

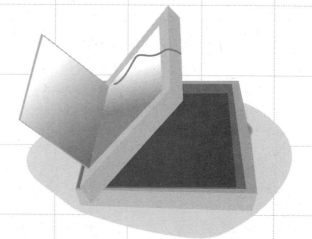

To Cook With Your
Solar-Powered Oven

1 Place your food inside the cooker. You can try using a graham cracker with a marshmallow on top or cheese on a cracker.

2 If you're using an oven thermometer, go ahead and put that inside your cooker as well. Close the box.

3 Put your cooker in a spot where it will get direct sunlight (driveways are good). Angle the top of the solar cooker so that the sun reflects off your aluminum-foil-covered lid and into the cooker. You want to make your cooker collect as much sunlight as possible. Use the ruler or other object to prop the lid open at the perfect angle. You may have to use tape to secure it if you have a bit of wind.

4 Check on your box in about half an hour to see how the food is progressing. Depending on the weather, it will take about twice the time to cook than in your regular oven indoors. Food will cook faster in the summer than in the winter.

Make Your Own
Pocket Sundial

Keep this sundial in your pocket and you'll always be able to tell the time using shadows cast on the sundial's small chart.

1 Photocopy the sundial chart from the next page. Color the different time periods in different colors to make it easier to read. When you cut it out, be sure to keep the overlapping space on the left side of the chart. You'll tape the chart over itself on this extra paper.

2 Hammer the nail into the dowel about ½ inch from the end. It shouldn't go in all the way; it needs to stick out to cast its shadow on the graph.

3 Wrap the chart around the middle of the dowel, and tape it securely to itself—not the dowel. You'll be turning the graph on the dowel, so it needs to be tight enough that it won't slip, but loose enough that it will turn. Move the chart up under the nail so it's just touching. If you want, you can put a thumbtack under the chart so it won't slip right off the dowel.

4 Screw the eye screw in the top of the dowel, and tie your string to it. Turn the chart so the current month is directly below the nail.

Supplies

sundial chart

colored pencils

scissors

4-inch piece of 1-inch-diameter wooden dowel (like from a broomstick)

hammer

1-inch nail

tape

an eye screw

string

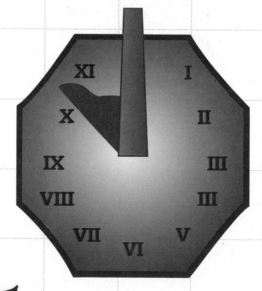

5 With your back to the sun, hold the sundial by the string and move your hand, turning the sundial, until the nail's shadow is pointing straight at the ground.

6 For the very first reading, you'll need to adjust your sundial. To do this, look at where the shadow falls and read the time on the chart. (Remember: each line represents two different times; if you're reading your sundial in the morning, use the first time. If it's afternoon, look at the second time.) Compare this to the time on your watch.

7 If it's different, you'll need to adjust the nail by hammering it in a bit at a time until it's accurately reflecting the time on your watch. You need to allow for Daylight Savings Time. During Daylight Savings Time add an hour. Otherwise your sundial will reflect the current time.

8 Once the nail is hammered in the right distance, you're ready to use your pocket sundial.

Photocopy the sundial chart below at 100%.

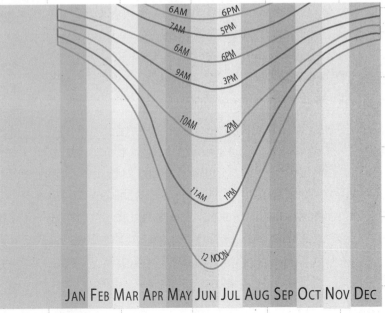

Make Your Own
Sunflower House

Create a natural hideaway using cheerful sunflowers as the walls. Sunflowers are quick-growing and fun to watch as they turn their heads toward the sun.

1 Find a spot to grow your house that gets direct sunlight. Outline the four walls of your house by digging small trenches. Don't forget to leave a space for the door!

2 Push the dowels or stakes into the ground in the trenches a foot apart from one another. This will be what your bean plants grow on, so plant the bean seeds close to the dowels.

3 Plant all of your seeds in the trenches according to the package directions. Try to mix them so that you have a good blend between beans and tall and short flowers. This will ensure you don't have any irregular gaps in the walls of the house.

4 Spread the mulch or hay on the ground where your floor will be (be careful not to cover your seeds). Or, you can just leave the ground as it is.

5 Water your plants regularly. When the beans begin to grow, tie them to the stakes to "train" them to twist their vines up the stakes. When they reach close to the top, tie string across the stakes, over your floor area, to create the roof of your house.

Supplies

shovel

dowels or planting stakes about five feet long. How many depends on how large your house will be. Plan for about one stake every foot or so.

packets of sunflower seeds: Try to get varieties of sunflowers that grow to different heights so you'll have solid walls. Some examples are: Lemon Queen (grows up to 8 feet), Autumn Beauty (grows 5–6 feet), and the Dwarf Sunspot (grows up to 18 inches)

bean seeds: use a variety that climbs, such as pole beans.

mulch or hay (optional)

water

string

Life
on Earth

Life is everywhere on Earth. No matter which biome you're in—blistering desert, frigid tundra, steamy rainforest—you name it, and life is there. Even in the most extreme conditions on the planet—riding the smoking hydrothermal vents under the sea or buried deep inside a glacier—there's life. It's one of the things that makes our planet unique in our solar system, and different life forms are a critical part of our environment.

Without one of the three crucial ingredients of water, air, or sun on Earth, life as we know it would not exist here. What's even more amazing is the diversity of life on our planet. All the creatures aren't the same—far from it. Each has different defenses, habitats, diet, and communication.

Classifying all the living things on Earth has fascinated scientists over the centuries. Back in the 1700s, scientists felt there were two **kingdoms**: plants and animals. Later, that expanded to three, then to six, then to a multi-tiered tree as scientists tried to find patterns between the vast differences in organisms.

Did You Know?

No one knows for sure how many **species** of plants and animals there are in the world. Estimates are just that—educated guesses. Some scientists believe there are around 10 million species. Others estimate there are up to 100 million!

As scientists learn more about unusual forms of life, such as viruses and other microscopic organisms, the kingdoms will undoubtedly change again. Why is it so complicated? It's like trying to organize everything in your house into a logical list. You'd have to find things that are similar by definition. But, some things can cross over into other defined groups. A pair of cotton socks could be grouped with "footwear," "cotton clothing," or "things that go in pairs," for example.

After classifying an organism into a kingdom, there's still more classifying to be done. Scientists break groups of organisms down further into more sections, each getting more and more specific until the particular species is named.

One thing they do agree on, though, is that all living creatures on Earth interact with each other and depend on each other for survival. Organisms are linked through the food chain, through sharing of a habitat, or **symbiosis**.

Words to Know

kingdoms: divisions of living organisms into broad categories.

species: a group of closely related and physically similar organisms.

symbiosis: a close relationship between two different organisms in an environment.

phylum: a related group descended from a common ancestor.

vertebrate: organism with a backbone or spinal column.

class: a group with common attributes; a major category in grouping organisms.

homeotherm: an organism that can regulate its own body temperature.

Getting Along

Plants and animals are connected through the food web, but some organisms have another way they interact with each other. Symbiosis is when two different species form a partnership with each other, often with mutually beneficial results—one helps out the other, and the recipient returns the favor. The honeyguide bird eats beeswax and bee larvae, but it can't tear open a bee's nest. A ratel, which is a badger-like animal, can, though. The honeyguide spots a nest and flutters around the ratel's head, getting its attention and leading it to the nest. After the ratel has torn it open and eaten its fill of honey, the honeyguide can have its share, too.

But animals aren't the only ones who can form partnerships. The acacia plant is a thorny plant growing in hot regions. Ants make their home inside the large thorns and eat the plant's sweet secretions. The payback? When other insects or herbivores try to eat the acacia, the ants swarm from their homes and sting the intruder. But the ants are smart: When bees come to pollinate the plant, the ants leave them alone, because the bees are helpful to the plant's survival.

Familiar Classes

The **phylum** of organisms you're probably most familiar with, *Chordata*, which is **vertebrates**, is broken down into familiar **classes**.

Mammals (*Mammalia*) are **homeothermic** vertebrates who nurse their young and have hair in some form on their bodies. A few mammals do lay eggs (they're called monotremes and include animals like the platypus and echidna). Mammals are found on every continent.

Birds (*Aves*) are homeothermic vertebrates who have two legs and lay eggs. The variety of birds ranges from the two-and-a-half-inch bee hummingbird to the ostrich, which can be up to nine feet tall. Birds, too, are found on every continent—even Antarctica.

Reptiles (*Sauropsida*) are ectotherms and most lay eggs. Because they need heat from their environment to help regulate their body temperature, they're not found in Antarctica, but they live on every other continent.

Amphibians (*Amphibia*) are also ectotherms and spend at least part of their lives in water. Like reptiles, they need heat from their environment, and Amphibians also live on every continent except Antarctica.

How Living Things Are Classified

Kingdom	Animalia	Animalia	Animalia	Animalia	Plantae
Phylum	Chordata	Annelida	Chordata	Chordata	Magnoliophyta
Class	Mammalia	Clitellata	Aves	Chondirchthyes	Magnoliopsida
Order	Primates	Haplotxida	Falconiformes	Lamniformes	Sapindales
Family	Hominidae	Lumbricidae	Accipitridae	Lamnidae	Anacardiaceae
Genus	Homo	Lumbricus	Haliaeetus	Carcharodon	Toxicodendron
Species	sapiens	terrestris	leucocephalus	carcharias	radicans
Common name	**HUMAN**	**EARTHWORM**	**BALD EAGLE**	**GREAT WHITE SHARK**	**POISON IVY**

As the classification gets more specific, you're zeroing in on the particular organism. The path to the organism's specific classification can be very similar. Compare the classification for a coyote and a wolf. Because these two creatures are so similar, their classification is virtually the same, too, right down to the species. Your pet dog's is even closer to a wolf's. A dog's classification is *C. lupus familiaris*, which means the dog is a subspecies of the grey wolf.

Coyote: Animalia > Chordata > Mammalia > Carnivora > Canidae > Canis > C. latrans

Grey wolf: Animalia > Chordata > Mammalia > Carnivora > Canidae > Canis > C. lupus

Common Pond Insects

Mayfly nymphs eat plants and algae; in turn, they're eaten by water spiders.

Water spiders make underwater bubble "webs" to carry air below the surface to breathe. Fish and frogs eat them.

Water fleas aren't the same fleas your dog may be familiar with. They're aquatic insects that eat algae.

Water mites look like spiders because they're part of the arachnid family, too. These insects suck the blood from fellow water insects just as water lice do. Their cousins, the water spiders, eat them.

Dragonfly nymphs are helpful to us because they eat mosquito larvae. Then, when they're adult dragon flies, they keep gobbling up mosquitoes, so these are definitely a great insect to see in your pond.

Whirligig beetles are smooth and oval-shaped, so they're perfectly designed for streaking through the water while staying alert with their four eyes—two that look up, above the water, and two that look down, into the water.

Food Chains and Webs

All animals on Earth have to eat other living things, whether it's plant life or animals. There's a pattern to what each animal eats. A mouse eats some berries, and then a fox consumes the mouse. A fruit fly eats ripe fruit, a spider eats the fruit fly, and a bird eats spiders. These "straight line" eating patterns are called **food chains**. When there's crossover between food chains, it's called a **food web**. For example, a wasp could also eat the spider, or a hawk could consume a mouse. Life on Earth is tightly linked through these food chains and webs.

Words to Know

food chain: the feeding relationship between plants and animals in an environment.

food web: a community of organisms where there are several interrelated food chains.

predator: any animal that lives by preying on—eating—other animals.

adapt: change to survive in new or different conditions.

All food chains on Earth start with the same thing: green plants, called the primary producers. Food chains begin with the blue-green algae in the oceans to tiny sprouts on the earth and go all the way up to the top **predators** like raptors, crocodiles, wolves, and great white sharks.

Adaptation

One of the many amazing aspects of life on Earth is how it's **adapted** to survive even the most extreme conditions. While there are some animals that haven't changed for millions of years—such as the crocodile, who has remained virtually the same since the age of the dinosaurs—there are other animals who have adapted over time, developing coat or skin patterns to blend in with their environment. Animals like the Arctic hare take on this adaptation seasonally, growing a white coat to blend in with the snow in winter and a reddish-brown coat for camouflage in the summer months.

Some plants have unique adaptations, too, for example, the interesting Venus flytrap and other carnivorous plants. The Venus flytrap grows in coastal North and South Carolina in the United States. Like other plants, it needs minerals from the soil. But the conditions in the coastal soil weren't sufficient to provide these. So, the flytrap developed its unique method of catching and eating flies to provide the nitrogen it needs.

Make Your Own
Pond Exploration Kit

Explore life in the water with this pond exploration kit. Using a dip net, scoop up tiny critters and pond life to examine close up, and use the underwater viewer to get a clear look at the habitat and residents themselves.

Underwater Viewer

1 Remove the lid from the coffee can. Use the can opener to cut the bottom of the can off completely so you have a metal cylinder.

2 Stretch the plastic wrap as tightly as you can across the top of the can, and wrap the rubber bands securely around the can to keep the plastic wrap tight. Make sure there are no holes in the plastic wrap so water won't seep in!

3 Wade out slowly into a pond (or you can kneel on the ground beside the water). Push your viewer down into the water as deep as you can without it filling with water. If you stand very still, you'll be able to see the world beneath the surface, which may consist of plants, fish, and other critters in their natural habitat.

Supplies
large coffee can

can opener

plastic wrap

rubber bands

Dip Net

1 Attach the handle of the kitchen strainer to the broom handle using duct tape. Tape it very tightly so it doesn't fall off. Fill your shallow container with some pond water.

2 Use your dip net to reach into the pond and gently scoop through the water. Try doing one sweep from the top of the pond, examine it, then do a sweep from the middle of the pond, and finally one from the bottom of the pond.

3 Let the water drain through the strainer, then gently tap the contents into your shallow container "catch basin." Examine the critters you've found.

Supplies
small kitchen mesh strainer

broom handle

duct tape

shallow container

magnifying glass or microscope

identification chart

53

Make Your Own
Mini Food Chain

Here's a way you can create a tiny food chain to watch a predator and its prey.

1 Using a sharp knife, cut the first bottle's top off 2 inches from the cap. Cut the bottom of this bottle off 1 inch down from the seam on the bottom of the bottle. Discard the top and bottom. Using a sharp pointed tool or nail, poke small air holes in the big cylinder you've created.

2 Cut the second bottle's top off 4 inches from the cap. Take the cap off. Using a hammer and nail, poke a hole in the cap, then put the cap back on. Cut the second bottle's bottom off right at the bottom seam. Poke small air holes in the bottom of this second bottle. Discard the middle section of the second bottle. Cut the third bottle's bottom off at the bottom seam. This bottom will be your base.

3 To assemble your mini food chain, first slide the top of the second bottle into the body of the first bottle. You may have to twist it a bit. If these two sections don't seem to stay together tightly, use wide tape to seal them together. When it's in, set this two-part combo into the base, which is the bottom you cut off the third bottle.

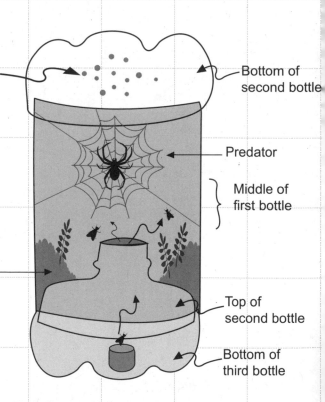

Air holes

Bottom of second bottle

Predator

Middle of first bottle

Soil/plants or twigs

Top of second bottle

Bottom of third bottle

Fruit flies go here; they fly up through the hole in the cap into the space where the predator lives.

4 Fill the container with soil, plants, and twigs. Put the bottom of the second bottle (the one you poked air holes into) on the top. Set this aside while you collect enough prey to sustain your mini food chain (see the next steps).

5 Take the last bottle and cut the top off about 4 inches from the top. Poke a very small hole in the cap big enough for a fruit fly to get through.

Supplies

four, 2-liter bottles with any labels cut off

sharp knife

small nail or small sharp tool

hammer

large nail

wide tape

soil, twigs, or small plants

empty film canisters

fruit, such as bananas

small plastic lid from a yogurt or margarine container

spiders

6 Put slices of fruit inside the empty film canisters. Set the small plastic lid in the base of your bottle to form a flat surface, and set your film canisters on top.

7 Turn the top bottle piece over and put it inside the bottom piece, forming a funnel into the bottom. Tape the top securely. Fruit flies will be drawn to the fruit, enter the funnel, and be trapped inside.

8 Find a small spider who's built a web around the yard and transfer it into your mini food chain environment when you've got some flies. To remove your flies from the trap, place the trap in the refrigerator for 30 minutes. This will slow them down so you can grab the film canisters with flies inside. Put the film canisters in the base of your ecosystem. They'll find their way up through the large hole in the cap, into the environment with your predator. Don't worry if you don't get lots of flies, though. They lay their eggs in the fruit. When the eggs hatch you'll have flies that way, too. Watch the interaction between predator and prey.

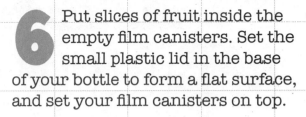

Flies enter here

Fly trap

Flies are attracted to fruit in film canisters

FOURTH BOTTLE

Make Your Own
Butterfly Feeder

Butterflies are some of the most beautiful insects. With this butterfly feeder, you'll be able to attract them easily.

1 Using the awl, poke four evenly-spaced holes in the clear plastic lid, about an inch from the edges. Try to make a diamond or square shape out of the holes so the string won't slip out easily.

2 Paint colorful flowers on the lid or use stickers. This will help attract the butterflies to your feeder.

Supplies

clear plastic lid, like the top from a deli container

very sharp awl or knife tip

paint and paintbrush or large, colorful stickers—flowers are ideal

twine or strong string

scissors

overripe fruit, such as bananas or oranges

3 Cut four equal pieces of string. The length depends on where you're going to hang your feeder. So, decide where it will be and then measure a distance that will let the feeder hang where you can see it.

4 Run each of the four pieces of string down through the holes you poked in the top of the plastic lid and knot them so they won't come back through the hole. Then tie all four pieces together at the top.

5 Hang your feeder from a tree or nail on the porch. Place the day-old fruit on it. The butterflies will be attracted to the color of your flowers and the overripe fruit.

Pollution

As you've seen, the environment is made up of systems, cycles, and specialized relationships between living and non-living elements. When everything's working the way it should, all the living organisms within the environment—including people—are healthy and thriving.

But when something harmful is introduced to the cycle, or part of the cycle is disrupted somehow, it can cause a chain reaction of problems right through the rest of the system. These changes can really hurt the health and well being of living organisms. One of these negative changes is **pollution**, which is the result of unnatural elements entering the environment. Unfortunately, humans are usually at fault.

Anything that's harmful to the environment is pollution—litter, car exhaust, motor oil, used tires, smoke, chemicals—all of this can have an instant or a gradual impact on the health of our earth.

Herbicides, meant to kill unwanted plants, and pesticides that kill insects, can enter the soil, water, and air, contaminating them and causing harm to living organisms.

It's kind of like an unhealthy diet. If you eat a lot of junk, your body just can't function the way it should. It's the same with the systems on our planet. But even though there's been a lot of damage done to the environment by **pollutants**, that doesn't mean it's "game over" for Earth. There are two ways to tackle the problem. First, clean up what we can. And second, take action to prevent further pollution.

Did You Know?

The most common garbage along highways comes from fast food wrappers.

Land Pollution

Most of the pollution on land comes from litter. People toss away garbage instead of disposing of it properly, which clogs up the land, attracts pests such as insects and rodents, and even harms the soil and the critters that live there if it contains chemicals. The majority of man-made objects can't break down over time, so they just lay where they've been left for years and years. If garbage kills the plants in an area by covering them up, it affects the food chain, since green plants are the start of every chain. It also affects the air quality, since plants help clean the air. If a material is made of an **organic** substance, it will **biodegrade**, but sometimes the process takes a very long time.

Did You Know?

In 2006, almost two million cigarette butts and filters were scooped out of the ocean in a coastal cleanup.

In just the United States alone, smokers consume over 300 billion cigarettes every year—and many smokers just flick their cigarette butts on the ground instead of disposing of them properly. Cigarette butts are the most common garbage in the United States! While the tobacco and paper parts of a cigarette break down, the plastic filters inside don't. They stick around the environment for years. What's more, marine and land animals mistake them for food and try to eat them—and die.

Land pollution is also a matter of sheer numbers. You may not think crumpling up a gum wrapper and tossing it on the ground is really that big a deal, but consider this: There are almost seven billion people in the world. If everyone drops one crumpled gum wrapper, there would be enough wrappers to go around the whole earth about seven times! And people are tossing a lot more than just gum wrappers on the ground.

Did You Know?

The chemicals in cigarettes kill the Daphnia, a microscopic aquatic animal that is important in the marine food chain.

Words to Know

pollution: man-made waste that contaminates an environment.

pollutant: any substance that pollutes, or dirties, the planet.

organic: something that was part of a living thing.

biodegrade: break down or decay and become absorbed into the environment.

Landfills

So, where does all the garbage we generate go? **Landfills** are areas where communities dump their solid waste. There are different kinds of landfills: some accept **hazardous waste**, some are "sanitary" landfills with protective barriers, and some are "**dumps**," with no protection for the environment or the living organisms nearby.

Did You Know?

In April 1815, Tambora Volcano in Indonesia erupted. It was the most powerful eruption in recorded history. Global temperatures went down as much as 3 degrees Celsius for so long that 1816 was called "the year without a summer."

Keeping the **Land Clean**

Easy things you can do that will help battle land pollution:

- **Keep a garbage bag in your car** to collect any food wrappers or other trash you accumulate while you're traveling.
- **Pick up and dispose of any trash you see,** whether you're hiking, riding your bike around the neighborhood, or vacationing at the beach.
- **Minimize the amount of garbage** your family generates by using re-useable containers, buying only what you really need, and giving away or donating items you don't need anymore rather than tossing them out.
- **Encourage** your school, local parks, or other places in your community to provide trash cans in convenient locations to make it easier for everyone to toss their junk appropriately.
- **Try to use natural methods,** rather than chemicals, to eliminate insects and unwanted weeds.

How long will it take to Biodegrade?

paper towel: about three weeks

apple: about two months

plastic bag: about 20 years

tin can: about 50 years

disposable diaper: over 400 years

glass bottle: about 1 million years!

Air Pollution

Some pollutants that enter the air come from natural sources. When a volcano erupts, for example, volcanic ash blasts into the air and can remain there for years. The larger the eruption, the bigger the cloud of ash and droplets of **acid rain** that enter the atmosphere. If the cloud is large enough, it can actually spread around the entire world and affect global temperatures. Other natural sources of air pollution include smoke from forest fires, and dust and sand from storms.

Airborne pollutants make it tough to breathe and can even cause diseases like cancer. One problem is the way winds criss-cross the globe, picking up pollutants and carrying them all over the world. This is how areas far away from where the actual pollution is created can become affected, too. Air pollution is not just a local concern.

While there are some natural sources of air pollution, the majority of air pollutants come from things we do ourselves—or things people have invented, such as the **combustion engine**.

The combustion engine uses fossil fuels. All living organisms are made up of the element carbon. Plants and animals that died hundreds of millions of years ago were gradually buried and exposed to heat and pressure for all that time. The heat and pressure fossilized these dead plants and animals into what we call fossil fuels—coal, oil, and natural gas. Burning these fossil fuels produces carbon dioxide, which contributes to the pollution in our atmosphere.

The problem is that humans have become completely dependent on fossil fuels. Not only does it hurt the environment when we use them, but they're also limited in quantity—there's only so much of them to dig up out of the earth. We use fossil fuels for more than just driving our cars. We use oil and gas to heat our homes, and coal powers some electrical plants. But burning all that fossil fuel is choking our atmosphere.

Remember the saying about **ozone**, "Good up high, bad nearby"? The ozone that's close to the ground is primarily formed by human activities (yep, burning those fossil fuels again!). When you see it in the form of smog, it can be harmful to your health. The amount of ozone can be so bad on hot days that health warnings actually advise people to stay indoors and avoid breathing in the polluted air.

Some elements of air pollution include:

- **Sulfur dioxide,** formed when coal and crude oil are burned. It enters the air and contributes to respiratory illness (like asthma), particularly in children and the elderly. It can also affect people with heart and lung disease.
- **Mono-nitrogen oxide,** produced by combustion engines, causing smog.
- **Carbon monoxide,** another product of combustion engines, which is toxic.
- **Particulate matter,** such as smoke and dust, which can come from many sources. Some of these sources are smokestacks and clear cutting forests.

Keeping the **Air Clean**

Air pollution can be reduced by taking action:

- **Turn off electronics and lights** when you're not using them. This is easy, and it really helps in the long run. Your home could be burning more fossil fuels than driving a car all over town!
- **Switch to compact fluorescent light bulbs,** which are 75 percent more effective than traditional bulbs. They last longer, too.
- **Ask parents to turn their engines off** in the carpool lane if they're waiting a long time. Have your school to pass out reminders to parents.
- **Help your parents plan errands** so you can get everything done in one trip instead of going out several times.
- **Ask your parents to use less air conditioning** in the summer or turn down the heat in the winter. Wear slippers or a sweater to stay more comfortable when it's chilly.

Did You Know?

Noise pollution is a very real threat to wildlife—very loud noises from machinery or vehicles can disrupt animals' migration and breeding and limit their choice of habitat.

Words to Know

landfill: place where waste and garbage is buried between layers of earth.

hazardous waste: garbage that is dangerous to living beings.

dump: a place where waste is stored without being buried.

acid rain: precipitation that has been polluted by acid.

combustion engine: an engine that runs on heat, either from a furnace or from inside the engine itself.

ozone: a gas that is a major air pollutant in the lower atmosphere but a beneficial part of the upper atmosphere. The ozone layer, which is located about 20 to 30 miles above the earth's surface, contains high levels of ozone that block most ultraviolet solar rays.

Water Pollution

When sewage, oil, chemicals, and other pollutants enter the water cycle, it can be devastating and even deadly. **Sediments** that collect in the water from trash or chemicals in the water prevent fish from filtering oxygen through their gills, and they can suffocate. When the dissolved oxygen in the water drops below a certain level (two to five parts per million gallons of water), many types of fish and aquatic animals can't survive. Aquatic plants also are "choked" and die, disrupting the food chains.

Pollutants can come from different sources:

- **Sewage and farm waste** can introduce harmful bacteria.
- **Herbicides, pesticides, and fertilizers** from agriculture can wash into the water. Industries sometimes dump their **waste water**, often containing acids, oils, harmful bacteria, and poisons.
- Beach-goers and boaters often leave their **trash** behind
- **Silt** from construction or land clearing sites can enter the water through runoff.

You probably remember that the water cycle includes the ocean, so pollutants that enter the water cycle can end up harming **marine life**, disrupting

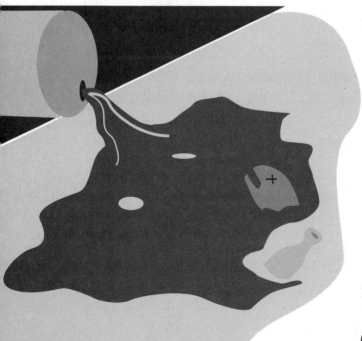

the marine food chain. What's more, the effect of any harmful pollutants can be felt all the way up the food chain. Suppose tiny copepods, which are small marine critters that look like a teardrop, absorb a pollutant into their bodies. A small fish can consume many copepods, making the concentration of pollutant greater in that little fish's body. Then a larger fish eats lots of small fish, and he has a higher concentration in his body, and on up the food chain.

In fact, this is how an insecticide was blamed for the decline in **birds of prey** in the United States. The birds were eating fish with high levels of the insecticide, and it made the shells of the eggs they laid very weak and thin. The eggs couldn't hatch, and the population of the birds dropped. Since the insecticide was banned, though, the birds have made a fantastic comeback.

Words to Know

sediment: material deposited by water, wind, or glaciers.

marine life: all organisms that live in the oceans.

birds of prey: birds that are predators, who eat other animals.

Acid Rain

When pollutants such as sulfur dioxide and nitrogen oxides enter the air, they join water droplets and form acid rain. Whatever acid rain falls on is affected in some way. The soil can become acidic, the water chemistry can change—acid rain can even wear away statues and rock! Historical monuments, old gravestones, and other building structures are permanently damaged by acid rain.

Acid rain can be deadly for some soil-living creatures, like the ones you may have spotted with the Berlese-Tullgren funnel, and some aquatic organisms. And that means—you guessed it—the food web is disrupted at the very beginning. Plants wither and die from the acid in the water and soil, and it can even weaken trees and make them vulnerable to diseases.

Try This

Drop a piece of chalk into a glass, then pour vinegar, which is acidic, to cover it. What happens to the chalk? The result is similar to what acid rain does to rocks and statues over time.

65

Oil Spills

When a massive amount of crude oil (dense, thick natural oil) is released into water because of accidents involving transport freighters, the marine life suffers greatly. Marine mammals and birds become coated in the oil and can't easily clean it off. Birds can't maintain their body temperature or fly when their feathers are coated in oil, and when they preen, they swallow the oil and die. It's so difficult to clean up an oil spill because the water currents carry the oil over large distances. It's also tough because scooping up oil from the water or cleaning it off of rocks or sandy beaches is an incredibly difficult job.

You can see for yourself how an oil spill spreads. Try tossing a handful of stale, unbuttered and unsalted popcorn into a natural body of water. Watch how quickly the kernels drift away from each other and around the water. You can imagine how a large pool of oil, floating on the surface of the water, can easily spread over a large area of ocean, riding the currents.

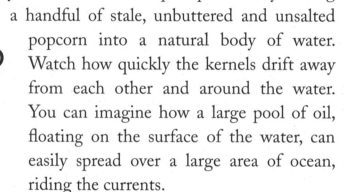

Try This

If you find a feather, look at it closely. You can see little "hooks" where the individual pieces of the feather cling together along the shaft. If you pull gently, you can separate them, but if you smooth it carefully, they'll cling back together. Now try putting a drop or two of vegetable oil on the feather. When you separate the feather this time, it won't go back together properly. That's what birds face when they're covered in oil from a spill.

Keeping the **Water Clean**

To help stop water pollution:

- Keep **oil and grease** out of storm drains.
- Use **flea combs** on your pets instead of pesticides.
- Tackle weeds the old fashioned way—**yank 'em out**.
- Be sure to **pick up** after beach visits.
- **Carpool** to school, take the bus, ride your bike, or walk.

Natural Repellents

Nature handles pests without all the chemicals—and we could learn a thing or two if we paid attention! Here are some natural ways to try repelling pests:

Catnip is 10 times more effective against mosquitoes than the chemical DEET.

Ladybugs are natural predators of aphids; encourage them to live in your garden.

Fill a zipper bag with water and hang it near entryways to discourage houseflies. Some people believe flies are scared away when they see their magnified reflection in the water.

Use herbal oils to repel mosquitoes, fleas, and ticks.

Got fleas? Set a shallow bowl filled with soapy water on the floor and direct the light from a desk lamp onto it in a dark room. The fleas will hop to the light and get caught in the soapy water.

Make Your Own
Chemical-Free,
Insect-Repelling Dog Collar

Rather than dousing your pup with chemicals to chase off fleas and ticks, try making a collar using some essential oils that have been found to repel insects. Don't use your collar on cats or young puppies, though. They may be too sensitive to the oils.

1 Trim at least three fabric scraps so they are about 2 inches wide, and long enough to go around your dog's neck with several inches left over. If you want a thicker collar, use six scraps; just layer two strips on top of one another when you braid them together. Lay all the scraps out in a row.

2 Fill the spray bottle with about two cups of distilled water, then add about 10 drops of each of your oils. Shake the spray bottle so the water and oil mix together.

3 Spray all of the fabric until it's damp, then leave it to dry. Once the scraps are dry, fold them in half the long way so you have long, thin strips, then use another scrap or some yarn to tie them together at the top so they stay folded.

4 Braid the scraps together. When you reach the end, secure them with another scrap or some yarn. Drape it loosely around your dog's neck and tie it together with another piece of fabric or yarn. You can also mist the spray lightly on your dog—be sure to keep it away from your pet's face so it doesn't get in the eyes or mouth—and rub it in with your hands.

Supplies

fabric scraps

spray bottle

distilled water

insect-repelling essential oils, such as citronella, eucalyptus, tea tree, lavender, peppermint, and catnip (at health or craft stores)

yarn

Make Your own
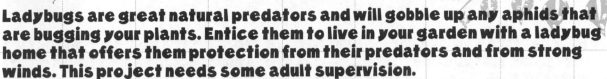

Ladybug Home

Ladybugs are great natural predators and will gobble up any aphids that are bugging your plants. Entice them to live in your garden with a ladybug home that offers them protection from their predators and from strong winds. This project needs some adult supervision.

1 Lay the container on its side. Cut a hinged "door" or flap on one long side of the carton by cutting around three sides. Fold the door open, and cut several slits (parallel to the ground) in the door. Make them between a quarter inch and a half inch wide so the ladybugs will be able to enter the house.

2 Cut three pieces of sandpaper, each about the size of one side of the carton. Using the door as access, glue each piece of sandpaper inside the house—sort of like sandpaper "wallpaper." This will give the ladybugs something to grab onto when they come inside. You can also glue sandpaper strips to the inside of the door, as long as you don't cover up the slits you made.

Supplies

empty milk or orange juice container (rectangular, waxed kind), clean and dry

sharp knife

sandpaper

scissors

glue

duct tape

contact paper, paint, or stickers

heavy stake, 2–3 feet long

ladybug attractant

3 Close the door and tape it shut. You can decorate the house any way you like, using stickers or paint. Contact paper in different colors cut in different shapes is also a fun way to decorate.

4 Mount your ladybug house onto a sturdy stake using duct tape. The slits should be parallel to the ground (this side should face out, not up or down). Stick the end of the stake into the ground near your garden so the house is about a foot off the ground. If you like, ask at your garden store for some ladybug attractant to put in your box to lure the little red beetles to their new home.

An empty wooden cigar box would also make a great ladybug house. You can use a Dremel tool (a rotary cutter found at hardware and all-purpose stores) to cut the slits in the lid. You won't need sandpaper. All the other directions are the same.

Make Your Own
Garbage

You may have to ask at your local hardware store or at a home construction site for some leftover PVC pipe and metal banding, but this project is worth the extra effort. Once you've made your own garbage picker-upper, keep it handy, along with a garbage bag, to pick up any stray litter you come across in your neighborhood.

1 Cut the PVC pipe into a 6-inch section and a 30-inch section (or however long you want your grabber to be). Put the PVC elbow onto the short section of pipe and set aside.

Supplies

Dremel tool

3/4-inch PVC pipe, about 3 feet long

3/4-inch PVC elbow

about 45 inches of metal banding, the kind that holds together lumber—ask at your local hardware store for some leftovers for you to recycle

duct tape

1/2-inch sheet metal screw (self-drilling)

screw driver

thick rubber band

2 Form a loop on one end of the metal banding and duct tape tightly. Your loop should be about 5 inches long.

Make a loop.

metal band   tape tightly

3 Using the Dremel tool, cut a 1-inch-by-2-inch rectangular "window" out of one end of the longer PVC pipe, starting 2 inches down from the end.

screw

Cut "window" wide enough for metal band.

4 Insert the screw about 3 inches down from the bottom of the rectangular hole you just cut. Don't put it all the way in—just far enough to be tight but still stick out. It's going to hold the rubber band to provide tension.

Picker-Upper

5 Thread the flat end of the banding into the bottom of the PVC pipe opposite the end with the rectangular hole. Pull it out through the rectangle hole. Stop when your metal loop is right at the bottom of the pipe. Connect the short PVC pipe to the top of the long one, using the elbow.

Pull metal band through.

6 Bend the metal banding as shown, making a little loop for the rubber band. The rest will be the handle that you'll pull. Bend the end of the banding so it's flat against the PVC handle and duct tape it very tightly. Cut off the excess banding and make sure you duct tape over the sharp edges so you don't cut yourself.

7 Cut the metal loop at the bottom in half to make two "grabbers." Bend them at right angles and put a little duct tape on the end of each so they're not too sharp.

8 Loop a rubber band around the screw, then through the handle, and back to the screw. When you hold the PVC handle, grab the metal handle and pull it. The "pinchers" will come up through the PVC pipe, closing—and picking up any litter!

Duct tape band to pipe tightly—be sure to cover edges so you don't cut yourself!

Loop rubber band around metal band and back to screw to provide tension.

Cut in half to make two "grabbers." Cover ends in duct tape so they're not sharp.

Global Warming

I f you've ever stepped into a greenhouse, you can understand what the buzz is all about when people talk about **global warming** and the **greenhouse effect**. The glass of the greenhouse allows the sun's rays inside, but doesn't allow them to exit as easily. The result? The temperature inside the greenhouse rises and the air inside is hotter than the air outside.

In a nutshell, that's what global warming is all about. Of course, there's no glass ceiling covering the earth; it's a bit more complicated than just comparing the planet to a glass house. After all, it still feels pretty cold in the winter, and the polar regions are still covered in ice, right?

OZONE

Global Warming

It's all about the global climate, not just how chilly it is or isn't in your backyard on any given day in January (or July, if you're in the Southern Hemisphere). Scientists measure the global climate by finding the average of temperatures across all regions of the earth, over all the seasons.

They've found this global temperature has increased 1 degree Fahrenheit in the past hundred years. Doesn't sound like a lot, does it? But even one degree of difference can start glaciers melting and animals migrating to adapt to changes brought about in their environment because of the temperature changes. Just one degree can change weather patterns and ecosystems. It can lead to extremes in drought in some areas, extremes in high rainfall in others. We have seen an increase in hurricanes because of warmer water temperatures, and hot, dry summers riddled with periods of drought. The earth would also experience increased flooding as land ice melts into the seas. What's more, if the trend continues as scientists predict, that one degree rise will turn into two degrees, then three . . .

Words to Know

global warming: an increase in the average temperature of the earth's atmosphere, enough to cause climate change.

greenhouse effect: when the presence in the atmosphere of gases such as carbon dioxide, water vapor, and methane allow incoming sunlight to pass through, but absorb heat radiated back from the earth's surface, trapping solar radiation.

greenhouse gases: various gases, including water vapor, carbon dioxide, and methane, that absorb infrared radiation, trap heat in the atmosphere, and contribute to the greenhouse effect.

Greenhouse Gases

Under normal conditions, sunlight radiates down to Earth and warms the land and the water, creating ideal conditions for life. Some of the energy is reflected back into the atmosphere, where gases called "**greenhouse gases**" trap some of that energy to maintain a comfortable living temperature on the planet.

We need some greenhouse gases for life to flourish here. In a healthy atmosphere, the rest of the energy is radiated back out into space. But when the greenhouse gases get too thick, very little heat can radiate back into the atmosphere, and our planet's thermostat starts to rise past a healthy level. And that's where global warming starts.

The earth has naturally occurring greenhouse gases, including water vapor, which have protected the planet throughout its life. And greenhouse gases like carbon dioxide, methane, and nitrous oxide are all naturally occurring in the atmosphere, too. But, human activity has added more of these gases into the environment than it can handle, making the atmosphere too clogged up for some of the radiation to escape back into space. The build-up of gases is what contributes to the greenhouse effect of rising temperatures.

Carbon dioxide is the biggest pollutant, primarily formed when we burn fossil fuels for energy, such as when we drive gas-powered cars. Carbon dioxide makes up the largest percentage of greenhouse gases. Some carbon dioxide comes from other natural sources, for example, when animals (and humans) breathe or when living things die and decay. But the majority of carbon dioxide in the atmosphere comes from other human activities. About one third of the carbon dioxide in the atmosphere comes from our sources of transportation—cars, buses, trucks, airplanes. A little less than one fourth of the carbon dioxide comes from lighting and heating our homes. The rest comes from factories and businesses.

Trees and plants take carbon dioxide from the air to use in photosynthesis. In a natural balance, everything would work out perfectly: animals would

Did You Know?

Poison ivy likes carbon dioxide. The more carbon dioxide in the environment, the bigger poison ivy grows. And the rash you get from it? Much more itchy!

74

breathe in oxygen and breathe out carbon dioxide, and plants would take in carbon dioxide, and return oxygen to the atmosphere. But when the balance is disturbed and there's far too much carbon dioxide in the atmosphere, our planet's **flora** just can't absorb it fast enough to maintain a balance. And that spells trouble for the atmosphere— and in return, trouble right here on Earth.

Words to Know

flora: plant life.

carbon footprint: the total amount of carbon dioxide and other greenhouse gases emitted over the full life cycle of a product or service, or by a person or family in a year.

That's why it's so important to keep our existing healthy trees and to plant new ones. The greener the earth, the healthier it will be.

Methane is the next most common greenhouse gas. Cattle are a big natural source of methane when they break down their food (and "break wind!"). With about one and a half billion cows in the world, that's a lot of methane! The biggest source of methane comes from landfills, where waste breaks down and releases the gas. It's also released during coal mining and the making of petroleum-based products.

Nitrous oxide is another greenhouse gas. It's produced naturally by bacteria in the soil. The human contribution to nitrous oxide comes from the use of nitrogen-based fertilizers. Although it's not present in such large quantities as carbon dioxide or methane, the chemical make-up of nitrous oxide makes it actually trap more energy in the atmosphere than carbon dioxide—almost 300 times more—so it's small, but powerful.

Aerosol cans, such as those used to hold whipped cream and cooking spray, need a propellant to squirt out their contents. Years ago, the propellants used were chlorofluorocarbons, or CFCs. These chemicals were found to weaken the ozone in the stratosphere. CFCs are now banned in spray cans and foam packaging, so aerosols use different propellants to spray—and one of those is sometimes nitrous oxide.

Did You Know?

One little critter is responsible for a whopping 11 percent of global methane emissions from natural sources: the termite.

75

Global Warming: Fact or Fiction?

Some people don't believe that global warming is the result of human actions. They think that it's a natural progression of Earth's cycles. There is evidence that the planet has cycled through many periods of natural heating and cooling. During the days of the dinosaur the earth was warmer than it is today and there were little or no polar ice caps. But scientists who believe in global warming point out that those cycles took place gradually. What's different today is that our recent warming has happened over a relatively short period of time—related to our heavy use of fossil fuels. Whether global warming is a natural cycle, a product of human activity, or a combination of the two, it's still wise to take steps to care for our planet and reduce our dependency on limited fuel sources.

What's Your Carbon Footprint?

How much of an impact you have on the environment—how much your activities add carbon dioxide to the atmosphere—is measured and represented in what's called a **carbon footprint**. The greater your number, the heavier your impact is, like a giant footprint upon the earth. Ideally, when people see, in plain numbers, how much their lifestyles are affecting the planet, they take steps to make changes and reduce that footprint. They start making choices that are gentler on the earth. The carbon footprint is calculated based on different factors.

What's Measured and Why:

Where you live. This probably determines how your home is powered. Depending on where you live, your home could receive electricity from coal, hydroelectricity, or natural gas.

How much electricity your household uses. Calculates the amount of power used.

How many people are in your family. Even sharing a household, more people in one home use more appliances and energy.

What kind of car your family drives and how far. Determines how much fuel is burned.

Airplane trips you take. Airplanes use a lot of fuel, especially on take-off. The more trips you take, the more fuel is being consumed to get you there.

Community Projects

Sometimes it's easy to think you can't make an impact on the world if you plant a tree or recycle a soda can. After all, you're just one person. It's just one tree. But think about what nature shows us: a nest of ants, together, can tackle a much larger invader and win! It's because they're working together, naturally. So consider getting a group of friends together, or a neighborhood or church group. There are lots of community projects you can organize to help the environment.

Restore wildlife habitat. Pick up the trash and replant native plants to encourage wildlife in neglected or unused areas.

Use school grounds. Talk to a teacher about a school-wide project. Build a pond to host local wildlife or a community garden to encourage people to cut down on produce they buy from faraway places. That food has to be shipped to your area, which uses fuel.

Take on the carpool. Sometimes parents wait for over an hour at school, idling their car engines and running the air conditioning the whole time! Pass out information about harmful car emissions, or brainstorm something parents can do inside the school while parked in line.

Create an errand pool. Coordinate an errand pool with neighbors to reduce the amount of driving everyone does. Families can take turns running errands or pick things up for one another to reduce special trips to the store.

Try This

Go online to one of the carbon footprint calculators and see how large your family's carbon footprint is. You can google "carbon footprint calculator" and choose one, or try one of these: **www.nature.org/initiatives/climatechange/** or **www.carbonfootprint.com.** If you try more than one of these you'll be surprised at the different results you get. Any ideas why this might happen?

Make Your Own
Global Warming in a Jar

Here's an easy way to see the effect of the sun's energy on air that's "trapped," versus heated air that can freely move around.

1 Place one thermometer in each of the jars. Leave one jar uncovered. Cover the second jar with plastic wrap, secured with the rubber band.

2 Set both jars on the white paper in direct sunlight. Be sure that the sunlight is not falling directly on the front of the thermometers—turn the jars away from the sun so the rays hit the back of the thermometers instead. This way, you'll be sure you are getting a reading of the air inside the jars.

3 The uncovered jar represents the earth with the proper amount of greenhouse gases, allowing extra heat to escape from the atmosphere. The second jar represents the earth with a layer of greenhouse gases that is too thick.

4 Check on the jars every 30 minutes, and record the temperatures. Keep recording as long as you can—all day if possible.

5 Compare the readings on the thermometers to measure the difference between the two "atmospheres."

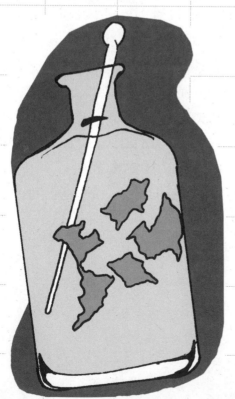

Supplies

2 outdoor thermometers

2 large glass jars

plastic wrap

rubber band

large piece of white paper

Propagate Your Own Tree

If you've got a favorite tree in your yard, you may be able to grow another one just like it by taking a "cutting" and planting it. You can give your new plants as gifts to encourage other people to plant more trees, too. This activity needs some adult supervision.

1 The best time to take a cutting from a favorite tree is early in the morning in winter when the tree is dormant. Willow trees grow quickly and propagate well whereas apple trees are a little harder. Ask a gardener for suggestions.

2 Clean the knife or pruning shear blades in rubbing alcohol to prevent disease from harming the tree. Cut off the end of a branch, about 4–6 inches long.

3 Remove leaves from the lower third of the cutting if there are any, and dip the cut end in rooting hormone. Tap off any excess.

4 Fill your container with a mixture of half sand, half peat. Insert the cutting about one third of its length into your potting medium.

5 Keep the potting medium moist by misting the plant on a regular schedule. You can cover the cutting with plastic to protect it, and place it in a well-lit area—but not in direct light.

6 In the spring, very carefully brush away the sand and peat to make sure your tree has grown roots. Transplant it into a larger container with soil. You may want to wait to transplant your tree into the ground until it's older and stronger to increase its odds of survival.

Supplies

established, healthy tree, preferably a species native to your area

very sharp, thin knife or sharp pruning shears

rubbing alcohol

rooting hormone, available from garden centers

coarse sand and peat

growing container, such as the bottom of an old plastic milk jug

Ozone
Depletion

Another environmental trouble that gets a lot of headlines is **ozone depletion**. You remember that ozone is a gas that's made of **molecules** formed by three oxygen **atoms**. The oxygen we breathe is made of two oxygen atoms. When it's close to the ground, ozone is toxic and unwanted, but up in the stratosphere, we need ozone to protect the earth from the sun's ultraviolet rays.

Did You Know?

"Ozone" comes from the Greek word meaning "smelly" because it has a very sharp odor.

Up in the stratosphere, ozone is naturally formed when the sun's ultraviolet light hits oxygen (O_2) in the air. The oxygen molecules split up, and the atoms rejoin as ozone (O_3) molecules. They're small but they're mighty, blocking harmful ultraviolet rays from reaching the earth.

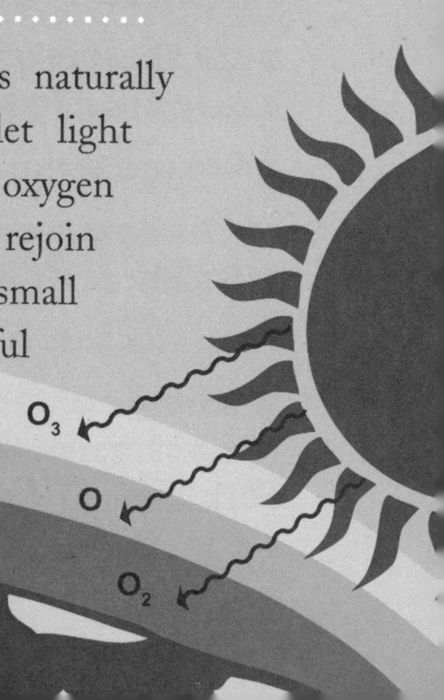

O_3

O

O_2

80

When certain gases, such as chlorine, enter the atmosphere, they tear apart the ozone molecules. The big culprits are **chlorofluorocarbons (CFCs)**, chemicals made of chlorine, fluorine, and carbon. When CFCs were invented in the 1930s, they were considered wonder chemicals. They were cheap and easy to produce, so CFCs were used in many different products, such as propellants in spray cans (like hair spray, bug spray, and deodorant) and to make foam food packaging and other things made from Styrofoam. By the early 1970s, however, scientists realized that those CFCs were floating up into the atmosphere, and what was happening up in the stratosphere was cause for alarm.

Simple Steps

Although you can't do anything about CFCs that have already been released into the atmosphere, there are steps you can take now to help stop any further destruction of the ozone.

Words to Know

ozone depletion: the thinning of the ozone layer.

molecule: the simplest structural unit of an element or compound. Molecules are made of atoms.

atom: the smallest particle of matter that cannot be broken down without changing the particle's properties.

chlorofluorocarbons (CFCs): simple gases that contain carbon, chlorine, fluorine, and sometimes hydrogen, that are a major cause of stratospheric ozone depletion.

Find substitutes for man-made products. Instead of foam "peanuts," try using the real thing—peanuts in their shells—or air-popped popcorn to protect your package. How about shredded or bunched-up newspaper or something else that's easily recyclable?

Use fans instead of the air conditioner.
Close the blinds on hot, sunny days to keep the heat out. Plant trees near your house to provide shade in the summer and protection from wind in the winter—not only will this help the ozone, but you'll also help fight global warming when your trees absorb carbon dioxide.

The "Hole" Story

The ozone layer surrounding the globe is getting thinner everywhere, but in some places it's worse than others. There's a significant thinning that occurs seasonally over Antarctica. It's not an actual "hole," really—just super-thin ozone, but it's referred to as a hole. During spring in Antarctica—September through November—up to 60 percent of the ozone in the stratosphere is lost above the big, icy continent. Why in the spring? During the winter Antarctica has the coldest temperatures in the world and receives no sunlight. Strong, swirling winds create clouds that release chlorine into the atmosphere. When the sun hits the chlorine in the spring, it goes to work tearing apart ozone molecules. Later as the winds calm and the temperature rises, the ozone grows thicker again. Scientists worry that more "holes" will open up in the ozone around the world, and that some day they may not thicken back up. Something similar happens in the Arctic polar regions. It's called a "dimple" since it's not as severe as Antarctica's ozone loss.

Did You Know?

One chlorine molecule can destroy up to 100,000 ozone molecules!

The sun's ultraviolet rays were breaking apart the CFCs and releasing the chlorine. That chlorine was "attacking" our protective ozone shield, allowing ultraviolet rays to reach down to Earth.

CFCs are tough stuff. They don't break down easily, hanging around in the environment for over 100 years. And CFCs take around 50 years to travel up to the stratosphere. Fortunately, CFCs were banned in 1978 in industrialized nations. Therefore, today's aerosol cans don't contribute any CFCs, and foam doesn't contain any CFCs either. But those CFCs released in 1970 won't even start attacking the ozone until around the year 2020.

SUN IS TOO HOT!

Ultraviolet Rays

Why are ultraviolet rays so harmful? You know the sun's light comes to the earth in the form of wavelengths that are invisible to the human eye—ultraviolet rays. There are two types of ultraviolet rays that reach the earth's surface, UVA and UVB. UVA rays penetrate the skin more deeply and can cause skin cancer. It's the UVB rays that cause sunburn. These rays can damage a protein in human skin called collagen, making your skin wrinkle as you get older. Too many rays in one day can cause serious sunburns, while skin cancer can develop from too much sun exposure over time. So, if the ozone in the stratosphere can't do its job and block the ultraviolet rays, people will have a greater risk of health troubles. Ultraviolet rays may also cause a gradual clouding of the lens of the eye, a condition called cataracts.

Did You Know?

Ultraviolet rays can damage your eyes, too. You need more than just sunscreen on your skin and a hat. Wear sunglasses to protect your eyes!

Humans aren't the only ones hurt by too much exposure to ultraviolet rays. Some types of tiny **plankton** can be affected by high levels of ultraviolet rays, either killing them or causing them to sink deeper into the ocean. Going deeper means the plant plankton won't get enough of the light they need to photosynthesize. And you know plankton are the foundation of the marine food chain. Any disruption to the plankton population means trouble for the rest of marine life—and humans, too.

Plants and crops can also be affected by harmful ultraviolet rays, although scientists are still studying the impact. Some types of plants are more affected than others—for example, one type of rice plant is negatively affected by too many UVB rays, but another type of rice plant doesn't show any signs of trouble at all.

Words to Know

plankton: the tiny plant and animal life that floats in bodies of water, such as algae, amoebas, and various larvae.

Make Your Own
Ozone Hole Magic Trick

When you're trying to explain the ozone problem to friends and family, try this magic trick to help get your point across.

1 Shape your modeling clay into a flat representation of Antarctica. Show it to your audience (whoever you're trying to teach about the ozone hole), and explain what it is, then put it in the bottom of your shallow dish.

2 Fill the dish with water, and explain to your audience this water is like the atmosphere that blankets the earth. Sprinkle the pepper into the water. The pepper represents the ozone layer—explain how it's made up of molecules of ozone, which is a combination of three oxygen atoms.

Supplies
modeling clay

shallow dish

water

pepper

liquid soap

3 Explain to your audience that years ago, CFCs were used in abundance in spray cans and foam packaging, and when those chemicals entered the air, they began a slow rise into the stratosphere. (You can even use your index finger to make a motion like you're spraying a can.) Say, "The result?" as you plunge your index finger into the water. The layer of pepper will fly away from your finger, creating a big "hole." Tell your audience, "The CFCs began attacking the ozone, creating a hole." Be ready to answer any questions about the ozone—but don't give away the secret of the magic trick!

Here's the secret: Before you begin your demonstration, carefully coat your index finger with soap. If you don't, the pepper will just gather around and stick to your finger—very unlike the ozone!

Did You Know?

Scientists measure the thickness of the ozone using weather balloons, high-flying aircraft, and satellites.

Nature
at Risk

Earth is the only planet in our solar system that hosts life in all its different, wonderful forms. As you know, however, all life is part of a big, balanced, connected system—if one part of the system is disrupted, the impact can ripple through many different parts of the web of life.

Unfortunately, it's human activity that causes the most problems in the environment. As the human population grows, we draw upon the land and its resources more and more, for food, fossil fuels, and space to live on. Our ancestors didn't realize just how delicate the environment is, so they made mistakes, such as over-hunting, or releasing harmful chemicals into the environment.

Words to Know

extinction: when a species no longer exists anywhere.

nocturnal: active at night.

And we're still introducing man-made products and waste into the environment. This can disrupt the environment and affect all kinds of species in negative ways if we're not careful.

Problems get magnified as time goes on, too. Overpopulation puts a huge stress on the planet's resources, especially if we're not careful about what we take and how we take it. If we catch too many fish from the oceans, pretty soon there won't be any fish left. If we keeping cutting down acres and acres of the Amazon rainforest every year, eventually we will destroy it completely. If we use too much water in areas where there isn't a lot of water, it won't be long before we use it all up.

Steps To **Extinction**

The path to extinction can be relatively quick or it can take a very long time. But, the end result is the same: as the saying goes, extinction is forever. Species can be classified according to how threatened they are. If experts determine a species of plant or animal is in jeopardy, they're placed on endangered status, depending on how many are left, and how great the risk is.

Rare: there is a relatively small number of individuals.

Threatened: the species probably will become endangered in the near future.

Endangered: in danger of becoming extinct.

Extinct in the wild: the only known individuals of the species are in captivity.

Extinct: there are no known individuals of the species left on the entire planet.

Human population growth shows no signs of slowing down, either. In the past century, the population has exploded—from around 1.5 billion people in 1900 to over six billion people on the planet by 2000! Experts predict that by 2050, the earth's population will grow to nearly nine billion. And all those people are going to need food, shelter, water, clothing, space to live, and lots of other resources.

But, the good news is this: As humans, we have control over our choices—what we eat, what we purchase, where we live, and how we dispose of our waste. If everyone does their own part to help protect the planet and all the species on it, we can work together to take care of our earth.

Understanding some of the problems some species face is the first step to helping out. And some species really need help— they're on the path to **extinction**.

What Causes Extinction?

There are different roads to extinction. An animal or plant may be exposed to any one of these, or more likely, several.

Excessive hunting. When the great auk, a large, penguin-type bird, was hunted in great numbers, even its eggs were prized and removed from the wild. The bird couldn't reproduce faster than it was being killed. In the mid 1800s, the last great auk was killed and the species became extinct. This is one way organisms become extinct—humans hunt them so aggressively that there's no chance for the species to repopulate fast enough to keep up its numbers.

Non-native species. You know every biome has its unique balance between climate, geology, and living organisms. When that balance is disrupted, it can mean the end for some species. That's what happened in the case of the birds of Guam. In the late 1940s, the tree snake arrived on the island, most likely as a stowaway on a ship. The bird population of Guam had never had to deal with snakes as predators, so they had no natural defenses against these tree-dwelling serpents. The result? The **nocturnal** snakes had an easy time catching the birds— and after about 40 years, there were very few birds remaining on the island, and

several species became extinct. Brown tree snakes on Guam aren't the only example, either. As humans have explored new territories, they have brought with them familiar animals to hunt for food, companion animals like cats, unwanted stowaways like rats, and seeds of non-native plants that invade the turf of native species.

Destruction of habitat. In the 1930s, the last heath hen died. The extinction was blamed partially on over-hunting and disease. A big reason, however, was the conversion of the heath hen's natural habitat along the East Coast to grazing land for cattle and settlements for people. Agriculture often takes over native habitats as farmers use land for grazing animals or planting crops. The timber industry cuts down acres of natural forests that are home to many species, too. A big concern is the loss of wetlands, as these areas are often drained or filled for city expansion, destroying entire ecosystems and the species that live there.

Did You Know?

Almost 2,000 plant and animal species around the world are threatened or endangered.

Food chain disruption. An organism can face extinction through an indirect route, too. The plucky little black-footed ferret, native to the American prairies, was declared extinct in the wild not once, but twice. The black-footed ferret depends on prairie dogs for food—a single ferret can eat up to 100 prairie dogs in one year. When people killed prairie dogs in massive numbers to use their habitat for grazing cattle, the black-footed ferret couldn't find food, died off, and was declared extinct. Years later in the mid-1980s, a very small group of black-footed ferrets was discovered, and these ferrets were brought into captivity to try to bring back the numbers. The black-footed ferret is an example of how easy it can be to impact one creature by hurting the population of another. It's like the domino effect—and when you consider a food web, the damage can be felt far down the line.

Did You Know?

Christopher Columbus may have dined on the Puerto Rican hutia, a rodent many believe is now extinct.

Natural extinction. Humans aren't the only reason species have faced extinction. Throughout the earth's history, climate changes and geological factors have caused the extinction of species, as well. The most talked about extinction, of course, was the disappearance of the dinosaurs. But there are other, less well-known examples of species going extinct in the distant past, too. Some scientists believe animals such as the mammoth, the dire wolf (a massive relative to modern wolves that stood five feet tall), or the giant Irish elk all went extinct because of changes in climate.

Some Endangered Animals

Some familiar and popular faces are on the endangered animal list. These large mammals are facing extinction if things don't change for them soon.

Polar bear: These big bears are abundant on logos and as cuddly stuffed animals. But in their natural habitat—the frozen lands of the Arctic—they're dwindling in numbers. As the global climate warms up, the land ice that the polar bear depends on is shrinking, putting this big mammal at risk.

Panda bear: The symbol of the World Wildlife Fund, the giant panda is a beloved critter. Only about 2,000 of these black and white giants still live in the wild. They've been hunted illegally for their beautiful coats, but there's another reason their numbers have dwindled. These giants munch on one particular kind of bamboo, and as the human population grows, their bamboo forests have been destroyed to make the land useable for people. Fortunately, people are working hard to save the giant panda, creating wildlife reserves to protect them.

Tiger: Another popular creature, this big cat is being hunted and pushed out of its habitat to the brink of extinction. Estimates suggest there are between 5,000 and 7,000 tigers left in the wild. Several **subspecies** of tigers have already gone extinct—a species of tiger in Indonesia went extinct as recently as the 1980s.

Asian elephant: Slightly smaller than the African elephant, the Asian elephant is at risk of losing its turf. Since it's a big animal—males can weight up to 11,000 pounds—the Asian elephant needs a lot of space to live and find food. As its natural spaces shrink, the numbers in the wild drop.

Give That Croc a Kiss

It's easy for people to get caught up in saving animals that we think are attractive, noble, or even cute and cuddly. But what about the ones that are down-right unattractive, or the ones that are deadly or fearsome to humans? These creatures need human help, too, if they're going to fight extinction. What's more, each of these animals is important to their ecosystem and to the earth as a balanced planet.

Top 10
Most Endangered Species

You'll see some of our planet's most beloved creatures are endangered—animals that are team mascots and featured on logos and in picture books galore. According to the World Wildlife Federation, the 10 most endangered species are:

1. Black Rhino
2. Giant Panda
3. Tiger
4. Beluga Sturgeon (fish)
5. Goldenseal (plant)
6. Alligator Snapping Turtle
7. Hawksbill Turtle
8. Big Leaf Mahogany (tree)
9. Green-Cheeked Parrot
10. Mako Shark

Words to Know

subspecies: a division of a group of organisms from the main species.

geothermal: heated internally from the earth.

finite: something that is limited.

sustainable: continuing something with minimal long-term impact on the environment.

wildlife refuge: an area of protected land where species can live away from human intervention.

hydroponics: growing plants in nutrient solutions without soil.

The saltwater crocodile can easily take down large mammals as its prey—even an adult water buffalo that's larger than a small car! Packing muscles and lightning reflexes into a streamlined body that can reach 20 feet in length, this reptile, with its gaping jaws lined with sharp teeth, would seem to be one tough critter. And yet the saltwater crocodile's population is at risk. Here's a fearsome predator that needs human help to avoid extinction.

And what about some other creatures that you never even knew existed, let alone realized were facing extinction?

Long-beaked echidna: This walking pincushion animal with a long, handle-like nose lives in New Guinea and is a special animal—it's one of the few mammals that lay eggs. Echidnas are hunted and have lost much of their habitat to logging and farming.

Northern hairy-nosed wombat: This Australian marsupial is one of the world's rarest mammals. Its stocky appearance and burrowing habits would lead you to believe it's a slow-mover, but it's surprisingly speedy, capable of running with its rolling gait up to 25 miles per hour. But this wombat is not fast enough to escape the non-native dingoes that hunt it. It's also dwindling because its herbivorous diet competes with that of introduced rabbits, cattle, and sheep.

Devil's hole pupfish: This small fish lives in a **geothermal** body of water in Nevada. Living in the desert, it needs to tolerate high temperatures—and it can, reportedly in water over 100 degrees! Land development in the desert pushed this little fish to endangered status in the late 1960s.

Plants don't escape the threat of extinction, either. Some species of cactus and lily are among the many plants that are threatened or endangered—again, mostly because of the loss of habitat as humans increasingly take over the land it needs.

Conservation and Preservation

Conservation and preservation involve protecting something, whether it's wildlife, plant life, a land area, or a natural resource. It's how people are trying to help the earth regain its natural balance. You've seen how fossil fuels—

like oil and petroleum—are being depleted by human activity and how they're a **finite** resource. When they're gone, they're gone. But fossil fuels aren't the only thing on Earth that's in danger of disappearing forever. Living organisms and entire ecosystems can be removed from the planet forever, too.

That's where conservation and preservation come in. Conservation involves reducing the stress on land and wildlife, and using **sustainable** management techniques. Preservation involves keeping land areas specifically for the use of the natural life within it. There are different ways people are helping save the endangered life on Earth. The best method involves protecting the species in its native habitat—by establishing an area as a **wildlife refuge**, or moving species to a nature reserve. Steps may be taken to stop an endangered species' habitat from being destroyed, and even rebuild the area. As a last resort, species are taken from the wild and cared for in another setting, sometimes in a zoo, to try to coax the species to build its numbers, ideally then returning it to the wild.

Did You Know?

President Teddy Roosevelt started the national wildlife refuge system in the United States in 1903.

When people save large land areas from human development, that's helping out tremendously, too. It keeps wild spaces available to the plants and animals that depend on it for their survival. Scientists are also trying to find new ways to increase food production for humans using less land. One way they're achieving it is through **hydroponics**, where plants grow without soil. The plants are given the nutrients they'd normally get from the soil through nutrient-rich water directly applied to their roots. This way, plants can grow in places that are already developed, reducing the need for more and more land devoted to farming. Plants can also grow hydroponically in less space—taking up vertical rows instead of horizontal rows.

Success Stories

Thanks to the efforts of caring people, there are success stories to report. Animals and plants have been removed from the endangered status as their numbers increase.

History has proven that when people decide to get involved and take action, species can be brought back from the brink of extinction—and even look forward to a very bright future.

From Extinction to Endangered: Przewalski's Horse, also called Mongolian Wild Horse or Takhi, was extinct in the wild at one point. Fortunately, there were several animals in captivity. Otherwise, these stocky, spirited animals would have been completely gone forever. However, in the 1990s, efforts were made to breed the remaining animals to build up their numbers, and eventually they were reintroduced back into the wilds of Mongolia. Although they're still on the endangered list, scientists have high hopes for the future of this horse.

Removed from the Endangered List in 2007, the national symbol of America, the American bald eagle, was removed from the threatened list in the United States. In earlier decades the chemical DDT had weakened the bald eagle's eggshells so much that they weren't hatching. After the eagle was placed on the list and protected by banning DDT, the bird was able to start successfully reproducing again and its numbers climbed.

Make Your Own
Hydroponic Planter

You can grow plants without soil when you create a hydroponic planter. You'll still need to find some kind of planting medium, but some scientists grow plants by spraying the nutrients plants need directly onto their roots. Have an adult help you with this project.

Supplies

2-liter bottle

scissors and sharp knife

strips of cotton rags or T-shirts

water

litmus paper to measure pH, availabe at garden, pool, hardware, or pet stores

lemon juice and baking soda

hydroponics plant nutrients, available at garden stores

planting medium, such as hay, pebbles, lava rocks, etc.

plants, try runners (like from a spider plant) or stem cutting (try something like an ivy plant), or if you want to start from seed, try lettuce or an herb like basil

aquarium tubing

small air pump or hollow rubber ball

1 Cut the bottle in half, leaving the cap on. In the top half, make a hole or slit big enough for a cloth strip to fit through. Thread the strip through so that some cloth is in the top of the bottle and the rest comes out the top of the bottle.

2 Fill the bottom half of the bottle with water. Use your litmus paper to test the pH of your water, following the included instructions on how to test pH. Plants need a pH of between 5 and 7 to grow well. If your water isn't in this range, add a little squirt of lemon juice to increase the acidity or a sprinkle of baking soda to decrease it. When your water is the right pH, add some plant nutrients to the water, using the instructions on the container to figure out how much you need. Set this aside.

3 Turn the bottle top upside down (be sure your cotton material—the "wick"—is still in place) and fill it with your planting medium. Tuck your plant runner or seeds in the middle of this material.

4 Set the top half of the bottle onto the bottom half. You want to be sure your wick is far enough in both the top and bottom halves to transport water up to the plant. Check back in a little bit to be sure that the water is, indeed, moving up the wick to the plant. Change the water about once a week, making sure the new water is the right pH and has plant nutrients in it.

5 Once your plant's roots start getting bigger, you can take the cap off and remove the wick, allowing the roots to reach down into the water themselves. If this happens, you'll need to oxygenate the water to prevent the roots from getting slimy. Cut a piece of aquarium tubing long enough to run down through the slit into the water. Either use a small air pump or a hollow rubber ball with the tubing poked into it for aeration. You'll need to "pump" the ball once a day to add oxygen to the water.

To Help Conservation

Eat more local foods. Visit a farmer's market, or plant your own garden. If you have a lot of space, try getting your neighbors together to plant a community garden where everyone pitches in to grow, care for, and eat the produce. When you eat local foods, you're reducing the amount of fuel used to transport food from other areas.

Purchase products that don't harm animals. That means no fur, ivory, or leather products.

Recycle, reuse, and cut down on unnecessary purchases. By doing all of this you reduce the amount of resources needed to make the stuff you use. This leaves more natural resources for the animals and plants who live there.

Support national parks and wildlife preserves. Visit or offer to volunteer however you can. Spread the word about these sanctuaries to get other people to understand and care about these treasured areas. There's at least one National Wildlife Refuge in every state in America.

Make Your own
Endangered Animal T-Shirt

When you wear your endangered animal T-shirt, you help draw attention to the plight of these animals. Your T-shirt will look like the animal is "fading" away—and you'll be helping raise awareness when anyone asks you about your shirt. Ask an adult to help you with this activity.

1 Do this project outside or in a well-ventilated area. Since you'll be using bleach, be very careful where you choose to work—outside on concrete is ideal. Have an adult help you avoid contact of bleach with your skin.

2 Lay your T-shirt out smoothly on a flat surface. Carefully place your insert between the layers of the shirt to block the bleach from penetrating to the back of the shirt.

3 Using a marker, draw a simple outline of your endangered or threatened animal on the sponge. Go to www.enchantedlearning.com/coloring/endangered to see pictures of lots of endangered animals. Cut around the border of your design with the scissors.

4 Put on the gloves. Fill the spray bottle with a couple of inches of bleach. You don't need to fill the whole bottle, just enough so the tube inside touches the liquid to spray. Pour about a half an inch of bleach into your shallow pan, too.

Supplies

solid-colored T-shirt

grocery bag, cardboard, or thick, old towels to insert inside T-shirt, something that can be ruined by bleach

marker

large, flat sponge

scissors

rubber or latex gloves

bleach

spray bottle

small, shallow pan

fabric paint

5 Spray the bottom half of the shirt with bleach—but be careful as you move upward toward the middle of the shirt. You need to spray a much finer mist the closer you go to the middle of the shirt. See if you can adjust the mister to allow a much lighter spray. If you can't, just minimize how much you spray. It's much better to spray less and add more later than to use too much at first. As you reach the middle, stop spraying, so you have only sprayed the bottom half.

6 Wait a couple of minutes to see the progress. You should have a gradual lightening of the shirt, with the whitest part at the very bottom.

7 When you're satisfied, dip your sponge animal cut-out in the bleach in the shallow pan. Carefully press your animal firmly in the center of your shirt, where you stopped spraying. Be careful not to jiggle the sponge too much, or it could turn out blurry. Hold it down for 30 seconds.

8 Lift the sponge off. Your shirt will show the silhouette of your endangered animal, gradually disappearing into the mist. On the back of the shirt, use fabric paint to draw your animal's footprint. Your shirt will show everyone who sees you that endangered animals could disappear from our planet, leaving only footprints behind.

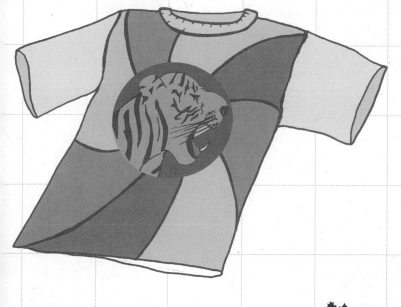

Make Your Own
Food Supply Experiment

As the earth's population grows, the pressures we put on the environment for food increases. You can see the results of this demand with this experiment, which uses yeast to eat the available sugar.

1 Measure ¼ teaspoon of yeast into one container, and add ½ cup of warm water. In the second container, add 1 teaspoon of yeast and ½ cup of warm water. Be sure the water isn't too hot or too cold—test it on the inside of your wrist. If you can't feel its temperature, it's perfect. Label your containers in some way.

2 Stir in 1 teaspoon of sugar into each of the containers and stir until the sugar is dissolved. Set the containers in a warm area, and check back every hour. Bubbles will begin to form. If the foam rises too high and threatens to spill over, stir it back down gently.

3 When the bubbles stop forming in one of your containers, make a note of which container it was. Note that it could be several hours before it stops bubbling.

4 Yeast are small organisms that use sugar as a food source and produce gas (the bubbles). The container that had the most yeast—a larger population—quickly ate through its supply of sugar and then ran out. The container that had less yeast—a smaller population— could continue to produce gas for a longer period of time. Think about what your experiment shows about large populations and existing food supplies.

Supplies
measuring spoons and cups

2 glass containers

yeast

warm water

sugar

Recycling

W hen something is used more than once, or when something old is used to make something new, that's recycling. Chances are, you and your family already recycle. Maybe you take a bin of newspapers down to the curb every week along with the garbage can, or you might take your recycling over to big community bins—usually dividing everything by type of material: paper, plastic, glass, aluminum.

In some places, you pay a deposit on a glass bottle or aluminum can and receive that money back when you return the container to the store. When you're recycling, you're taking steps toward helping the environment—but did you ever wonder how?

Recycling helps reduce the amount of garbage that ends up in landfills. It also reduces the amount of new material that needs to be used to make more things. When you recycle, you're saving the materials new goods are made from, and you're also saving the energy that would be needed to make those new materials. So recycling helps the environment in lots of different ways: by saving natural resources such as reducing the amount of trees that need to be cut down to make new paper; by reducing global warming because less fossil fuels need to be burned to produce those new materials; and by saving the land—by keeping that material out of the landfills.

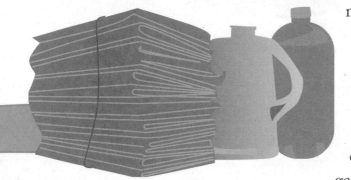

You've seen why it's important to cut down on the amount of garbage going into landfills, and you know why it's important to cut down on how much we burn fossil fuels. Recycling is one of the best ways to cut back on all that garbage.

Where Does It Go?

What happens to the recycling after you drop it off? All the material goes to a facility to be cleaned and sorted, then it heads to processing plants where each of the materials goes through a process that will make it available again to manufacturing plants—to be turned into new products.

Plastic. Plastic undergoes a multi-step process to become useable again. First the plastic is cleaned well to remove any debris, shredded, and washed again. The flakes are melted and extruded into strands, like plastic spaghetti. The strands are cooled, then chopped into pellets and sold to manufacturing companies. Lots of things are made from recycled plastic, even clothing!

Paper. When paper is recycled, it's broken down into a pulp and usually mixed with fresh wood pulp. It's hardest to recycle colored paper, because it must be "de-inked," or have the color removed. Paper can't be recycled forever—the fibers get weak over time, and new wood pulp has to be added in.

Did You Know?

Today, the United States recycles almost a third of its waste— almost twice as much as in the early 1990s.

Glass. One of the best recycling materials, glass can be re-used over and over. An exception is colored glass, because the color can't be removed, so clear glass is the best. When glass is recycled, it's crushed and re-melted to make new glass. To help the recycling process, remove paper labels from your glass jars before recycling them.

Metal. As with glass and plastic, metal is melted when it's being recycled. Then it's rolled out into thin sheets to be made into new products—for example, aluminum cans. It takes far less energy to recycle cans than it does to make new cans from fresh resources.

Other Ways to Recycle

Reuse. Sometimes you don't even realize how much stuff you toss into the trash every day. Truth is, in the United States, each person throws out an average of four and a half pounds of garbage every day! The next time you're about to toss something in the garbage, think about it: Is this something you could possibly use again, for another purpose? Many of the projects in this book can transform used items into something new. Save small containers and use them to sort small desk or kitchen objects. Use an old, punctured hose to water your garden. Take old milk jugs, cut them, and use them as shovels at the beach. Wash glass food jars and use them to store bulk foods or all those stray pennies, or to make decorative sand art jars for your home or for gifts.

Compost. Build a compost bin in your backyard to take on the "brown" and "green" waste from your household. Brown waste includes paper products like newspapers, shredded cereal boxes, and cardboard. Green waste is stuff like grass clippings, leaves, and food waste. You can compost almost all of your food waste, except for meat.

Pre-cycle. Take a good look at purchases you make before you make them. Is there excess packaging that you could avoid by buying something else? Choose something wrapped in paper over plastic or foam, because paper can be composted. Could you buy a larger size of a product and share it with neighbors, friends, or family, reducing the number of smaller packages that would have to be purchased to get the same amount of that product? And even consider if you really need the item at all, or can make do with something you already have!

Reduce Waste

Just how much garbage does your family generate? Make a chart to find out, recording the weekly weight of your trash. Record the weight of what you recycle as well. Then talk about the results with your family. How much of that trash can you recycle? Even better, how much can you reuse? You can even issue a challenge to family members to see who can generate the least amount of trash and make individual charts. See how your family can reduce its waste over time.

Look at how the choices you make affect your family's garbage output. For example, one box of microwave popcorn may have eight individual bags of popcorn—and each of those bags also has a plastic wrapper. Just counting pieces of material, that's 17 pieces of garbage to throw out! If you buy popcorn kernels instead and air-pop them or even do it the "old-fashioned" way, on the stove in a pan with oil, you'll just purchase the one bag of kernels—and you'll probably get far more than eight servings out of it, too. Microwave popcorn is just one example. There are plenty of examples you can find all around your kitchen, like frozen dinners or single serving snacks.

Pre-cycle Ideas

- If you **carry your own canvas shopping bags** into the store, you'll walk out with fewer plastic or paper shopping bags (or none at all!).
- **Take fabric scraps** and hem along the edges **to make cloth napkins** to use instead of paper products. This is actually recycling, too!
- **Use kitchen rags** instead of grabbing—and tossing—paper towels. This is another idea that's both pre-cycling and recycling!
- **Purchase rechargeable batteries.**

All In the Name of
Science

How would you like to have the job title, "garbologist" on your business card? Since the ending "-ologist" means someone who studies something, a "garbologist" is someone who studies garbage. Although it's not a formal job title, there are scientists who study the garbage a society produces in order to learn more about that society. Much like an anthropologist can learn from ancient civilizations based on what discarded artifacts they find, modern "garbologists" can learn about what we throw away—and how much of it.

In the oceans, there are swirling patterns of currents that form "gyres," like a whirlpool. Garbage that's been tossed overboard or swept out to sea can collect in these currents. Some garbologists scoop pounds of this garbage out of the waters to clean up the ocean and see what's being discarded. It's usually mostly floating plastics. Often, these plastics end up in the stomachs of marine birds and mammals, who have mistaken them for food. Another floating plastic danger is the rings that hold six-packs of beverages. Animals can easily get their necks caught in these— so if you absolutely must purchase drinks with these rings, you should snip all the rings free when you're finished.

Did You Know?

The red wiggler worm is most often employed in composting bins. It's different from your average earthworm-it loves rotting vegetation and compost, but doesn't do too well in "regular" soil. Your average earthworm, on the other hand, loves plain old soil!

Recycling in Nature

You know that there are many cycles in nature that move material through different steps—like the water cycle: Water evaporates into water vapor, rises up to the atmosphere, falls back to the earth, and is used by living organisms before it's returned to the water cycle. But, there is more recycling in nature, too. The organisms that live close to the ground—insects, bacteria, fungi, and earthworms—go to work breaking down everything from living remains to logs to even some garbage people have left behind.

Words to Know

compost: a mixture produced by decomposition of organic matter in a compost pile, used to fertilize the soil in the garden.

vermicomposting: raising worms to break down organic materials.

Insects and earthworms can eat organic material such as dead creatures and plant materials. They produce fertile soil as their waste products after they've digested them. This helps the environment not only by getting rid of dead organisms, but also by creating renewed soil for new organisms to grow in.

Fungi (for example, mushrooms, mold, and yeast) and bacteria break down plant matter through a chemical process. This reduces the organism to smaller components that can also be absorbed back into the soil, replenishing the environment and providing new materials for growing organisms.

Worms are one of the best recyclers, turning food waste into composting material to rebuild the soil. In fact, many people use **vermicomposting** as a way to reduce household waste. Large bins contain bedding and worms, and people add food waste for the worms to eat and break down. Some people even keep these containers right under the kitchen sink for convenience! It's similar to outdoor composting. But it's not smelly and doesn't attract insects if you put the proper waste materials in and maintain it properly.

Make Your Own
Naturally Dyed Shopping Tote

Ask your local grocer if he or she has any produce that needs to be thrown away—you can use it to make this shopping tote. (Just be sure not to eat any of it, even if it looks like it's okay!) Give anything you don't use to your worms to compost in your worm castle.

1 Crush or tear the plant material into small pieces. Put the pieces in a pot (one for each color) and add enough water to just cover them. Press down on the onion skins until they're compacted at the bottom of the pot.

2 If you're using crock pots, turn them on low and let them sit overnight or for several hours. If you're using regular pots, put the heat on low for several hours. Don't let them simmer, or the water will evaporate.

3 Let the liquid cool, then strain out the plant material over a bowl or other container. You'll be left with a natural, concentrated color dye.

4 You can use the dyes to create a tie-dye pattern on your canvas tote, dip stamps into the dyes and paint on your bag, or use a paintbrush to decorate. Let the tote dry completely before using. Use leftover dye to decorate an old T-shirt or create a fun towel for the beach.

Supplies

plant material for dyes such as grass cuttings, beets, the papery outer skin of onion peels, blueberries, or other materials

pots or crock pots

strainer

bowl or other container

canvas tote bag, white or off-white work best

brushes, stamps

Make Your Own
Worm Castle

Worms can eat your leftover garbage, turning it into rich soil to use in the garden. Be sure to keep your worm castle in a place that's warm and dark.

1 Cut a few inches off the top of the bottle, and put it aside for later. Tear or cut several pages of newspaper into strips about 1 inch wide. This is bedding material for your worms, and they'll break this down, too. Put some into the bottom of the bottle and lightly spritz them with water. You want them damp, but not soaking wet, or the worms will drown. Fill your bottle about half full with fluffed up, damp newspaper strips.

2 Add a cup full of soil and toss that with your newspapers, too. Put your worms into their castle, and when they've moved down away from the light, add some kitchen scraps and place a shallow layer of newspaper bedding material on top.

3 Poke several good-sized holes in the saved top of the bottle, and tape it on top either in an upright position or upside-down, whichever is more convenient for you. You need to be sure that enough air circulates inside your worm castle—this is worm composting, not a terrarium!

4 Keep your worm castle out of the light. Lay the construction paper out on a table, and cut along the long side to make notched "turrets" like you'd see on a castle. Your worms deserve a fancy place to live, after all.

Cut out a few window flaps—but only cut around three sides of the windows, so you can close the flaps when you're not observing your worms. When you're finished, wrap construction paper around the bottle tightly and tape it securely. The turrets should be at the top of the bottle.

5 Check regularly to see that the bedding stays just barely moist, and if the worms need new scraps. The worms will work on the food scraps and turn them into compost.

6 If you're going to maintain your castle for a long time, you'll need to remove the compost after a while. You can lure the worms to one side of your container by putting their food on one side, waiting a day or so for them to move over, then scooping up the compost. Replace the compost with fresh bedding. Also, keep an eye on the moisture in the bin. If it's getting too wet, poke a couple of small holes (too small for your worms to crawl out of!) in the bottom of the bin and set it in a saucer or container to catch any drips.

Supplies

2-liter plastic bottle

scissors

newspaper

spray bottle of water

soil

red crawlers, from a bait shop

kitchen scraps, see list for good choices

black construction paper

tape

Worms **Enjoy**

coffee grounds

fruits

vegetables

egg shells

used tea bags

Worms **Don't Enjoy**

meat, including fish

dairy products

non-foods like plastic

banana peels and oranges

bread

Make Your Own

Scratch-and-Sniff Recycled Paper

It's fun to make recycled paper, but it's even more fun to make scented paper! You can use this as writing paper or to give as a gift. Caution: don't pour shredded paper and water down the drain.

1 Shred the newspaper into small pieces and put about one cup of the shreds into a blender. Add about ¾ cup of water, then keep alternating layers of shredded paper and water until the blender is about half full. Turn the blender on low speed until everything's all mashed together and it looks like pulp. Add more water if the blender's getting bogged down.

Supplies

lots of newspaper, or other used paper

blender

water

spices or extracts for scents, such as cinnamon, vanilla, peppermint

large old towels or rags

two old pieces of window screen

2 Add your scent. Use about 4 drops of liquid extract or 2 tablespoons of solid spices, then blend again for a couple of seconds to mix it all together.

3 Take your mix outside. On a flat surface, spread out a large towel or rag. Lay one of the screens on top, then pour out your paper pulp onto the screen. Spread it evenly over your screen with your fingers, leaving a border of a couple of inches of screen all the way around the edges.

4 Lay the second screen on top so the pulp lays between the two screens, and press evenly around the entire surface to push water out of the pulp. If your towel gets saturated, carefully lift off your screen-and-paper "sandwich" and use a new towel to absorb the water. When most of the water is squeezed out, lay the whole thing out on another towel in a warm place to dry overnight. When it's dry, you can cut your paper into whatever size pieces you want.

The Balance of the Environment

The environment is an amazing, constantly changing place. It's incredible to think about all the elements that have to come together to make a functioning, highly interacting planet like Earth. And although picturing the earth as a balance isn't too far off the mark, it's more complex than just finding a simple good-versus-bad ratio.

Some things that might be good (like water) can turn, by a twist of nature, into something unpleasant (like a flood).

But even things that may seem harsh, like a wildfire, can turn out to be good for nature. In some areas, such as the western United States, wildfires are important in nature's cycle because they eliminate overgrowth by burning it and spark new growth with what's left behind.

What's really amazing is to realize just how much of an impact humans can have on the environment—for better or for worse. With just one discovery or one invention, we can damage the path our environment is taking. But just like in nature, there's a good side to invention, as well. Humans can also create things that are helpful to the environment or that heal the damage they've done to the environment. And what's even more empowering is that everyone can make choices and changes in their own lives that can make a lasting impact on our environment.

Learning about the challenges our environment faces shouldn't be all doom and gloom. As scientists and politicians learn more, countries are coming together to protect our planet by passing laws against dangerous practices and taking steps to manage our natural resources and protect what we have. Everyone plays a part in that process, so by learning all you can, you're already helping.

One of the most fun ways to get out and explore the natural world is by **geocaching**. With the help of a hand-held **Global Positioning System** (GPS), you seek out "caches," or treasure boxes, that other geocachers have hidden—all over the world!

Usually these caches are in natural settings, so if you start searching for them, you'll find yourself in parks and natural areas that you may not have even known were in your own community. And at the end of your trail is a real treasure, which is pretty cool, too! The best part: geocachers have made a pact with the environment. They don't hide boxes in areas that are disruptive to nature, and they have a "cache in, trash out" policy, which means they go hiking looking for treasure, but along the way they clean up any litter that others have left behind. It's a great way to experience nature and help out at the same time.

When you're out treasure hunting, take time to look around and observe the environment—look for signs of wildlife, study the kinds of plants that are native to your area, and look for any signs of impact by humans that can be corrected.

The more you explore and enjoy the nature in your own community and learn about it, the better you'll know how to care for it. And, luckily for you, there are tons of opportunities and places to go that let you do just that. Share your information with everyone you can—even though one person can have an impact by making changes, getting more people to care about our environment can really make the earth shine.

Words to Know

geocaching: an outdoor treasure-hunting game using navigational techniques and clues to hide and seek containers called "geocaches" or "caches." A cache generally contains a logbook and "treasure," such as toys or trinkets.

Global Positioning System: a system of satellites, computers, and receivers that can determine the exact location of a receiver anywhere on the planet.

Make Your Own...
Environment Charm Bracelet

Wear your Earth pride on your wrist with this unique charm bracelet—or make two and share one with a friend.

1 Measure two pieces of string, a little longer than the length you want the finished product to be. Wrap the string one-and-a-half times around your wrist and cut the string, then cut another string the same length. Measure two other pieces about five or six times longer than you want the finished bracelet to be. To do this, wrap the string around your wrist five or six times and then cut the string. Then cut another piece of string the same length.

2 Lay all four pieces out on your work surface, putting the two longer pieces (A and B in the diagram) in the inside positions. Knot all four strings together at the top, then be sure they're all in the proper position again before you start. Tape the knot to you work surface to hold it in place.

Supplies

hemp string

scissors

tape

colored polymer clay

small paper clips

small key ring—type loops, from the jewelry section of a craft store

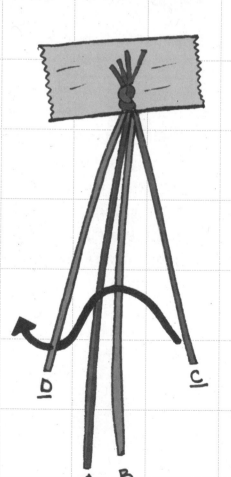

3 Take the right string (C in the diagram) over strings A and B and under the left string (D in the diagram). Let go of it for a minute and let it lay loosely where it is, under the left string. Pick up string D and bring it under strings A and B, then up and over string C. Tighten the knot and push it to the top by pulling on strings C and D.

4 Now you're ready to make a second knot. Your outside strings (C and D) have changed positions. Fold string C (now on the left) over strings A and B and under string D. Let it lay loosely. Bring string D under strings A and B and up and over string C. Tighten this knot all the way to the top.

5 Continue making knots, alternating directions back and forth across the middle strings, until your bracelet is as long as you want it to be. When it's finished, tie a knot in the end and set it aside.

6 Using the colored polymer clay, make small charms for your bracelet, making symbols to reflect the environment. Some things to try: your favorite endangered animal, the sun, the earth, a water drop, a green plant, a worm from your compost bin! Be sure you make your charms a reasonable size for your bracelet but large enough to cover most of a paper clip. When you're finished, take the small paper clips and press them gently into your charms until the paper clip is almost completely buried. Be sure to leave one small end sticking out. This will be where you connect your charm to the bracelet. Bake the charms according to the directions on the package.

7 In the meantime, take the small key ring loops and carefully turn them through your bracelet at even intervals. You can push them right through the strings so they stay where you put them. When your charms are cool, attach them to your bracelet by turning the key ring loops through the paper clip ends.

Make Your Own
"Bring the Earth

Ready to save the earth? Play this game with your friends, and you can test each other to see how much you know about our planet and how to care for it

1 Set up the scale. If you've made your own, hang it from a place where it can move freely (such as from the light over the kitchen table) or put a dowel horizontally on a table with one end hanging off it and set some heavy books on top of it. Then you can hang the scale from the dowel.

Supplies

balance scale (see next page)

question cards (see next page)

items to represent parts of the environment and man-made elements—these are all things that impact the environment, for example: small metal vehicles, small plastic animals or plants, small balloons filled with air, pill containers filled with water, pieces of paper for "garbage," and small rocks

one die

very small objects to use as markers—you can use uniform-sized counting markers, pieces of cardboard, small stones, etc.

2 Load up one container of the balance with the things you've gathered that are impacting the environment. Your scale will now be off-balance. It's up to you to bring the environment back into balance.

3 Begin play by rolling the die. If you roll a one, pick a card from the earth pile. A two is a card from the air pile, a three is a card from the water pile, and so on. If you answer the question correctly, put a marker in the "healthy earth" side of the scale (the one that started out empty). If you answer incorrectly, the next player goes.

4 If someone rolls a six, that's not good news for the earth—a marker goes into the "unhealthy Earth" side of the scale, the side that started out with all the elements piled in it.

5 You and your friends are successful when the balance is brought back to the planet.

Back Into Balance" Game

Balance Scale

1 Squeeze the coat hanger so it's less like a triangle and more like a squished curve.

2 Using the hole punch, make three evenly spaced holes around the rims of each plastic container.

3 Cut six pieces of string exactly the same length—about a foot long each. Tie one end of each string to one hole on each of the containers.

4 Gather the ends of the three strings from one container and tie them in a knot to one end of the coat hanger. Do the same with the second set of strings and container, securing this one to the other side of the coat hanger.

5 Balance the hook of the coat hanger on your finger to see if it's equally balanced. If it's not, slide the string of one container or the other along the coat hanger until they're balanced. When you find the perfect place for each container, secure it there with tape.

Supplies

metal coat hanger

two identical thin plastic containers

single hole punch

scissors

string

tape

Question Cards

Question cards can be true or false questions, multiple choice, or just one-answer cards. It's up to you how you'd like to do them.

1 Take 50 index cards and divide them into five piles. Each pile will represent one of the following categories: earth, air, water, sun, or life. Decorate your cards.

2 Write a question about the environment on each card that involves that category— a fact or information involving the environment. Go through this book or go to some of the websites listed in the back to get ideas. Here are some to get you started with the answers in parentheses.

Supplies

index cards

markers

EARTH

1. How much of the planet is made up of the desert biome? (one-fifth)
2. True or false: biomes always stay the same through time—once a forest, always a forest. (false)
3. What is climate? (the weather conditions that are typically found in a geographical area)
4. True or false: Penguins are only found in snowy climates. (false—some penguins live in warm coastal climates)
5. True or false: Tiny living organisms live in the ground. (true)

AIR

1. What element is air mostly made of? (nitrogen)
2. What's the name of the lowest layer of the atmosphere? (troposphere)
3. What's the saying that tells us which ozone is "good" and which is "bad"? (good up high, bad nearby)
4. True or false: Winds always blow in the same direction. (false)
5. True or false: Fish breathe oxygen, too. (true)

WATER

1. True or false: Most of the water on Earth is freshwater. (false)
2. How many oceans are on Earth? (five)
3. What is salinity? (the amount of salt in a solution)
4. What are the largest bodies of water on Earth called? (ocean)
5. In what frozen mass is most of the Earth's fresh water locked? (glacier)

SUN

1. True or false: The sun is solid. (false—the sun is made of gases)
2. True or false: Our sun is the largest star in the universe. (false)
3. What kind of ultraviolet rays cause sunburns? (UVB)
4. Is it hotter on the surface of the sun, or on the inside? (inside)
5. What prevents some of the sun's heat from escaping back into space after it comes to Earth? (greenhouse gases)

LIFE

1. What class do you, a dog, and a whale all belong to? (mammalia)
2. What's it called when an organism changes over time to be better suited to its environment? (adaptation)
3. List two tiny creatures that live in a pond. (could be: nymphs, water spiders, water fleas, water mites, beetles, etc.)
4. What animal was taken off the endangered list in 2007? (bald eagle)
5. Who started the National Wildlife Refuge system in the United States? (President Theodore Roosevelt)

Glossary

acid rain: precipitation that has been polluted by acid.

adapt: change to survive in new or different conditions.

Antarctic Circle: the invisible ring around the southern part of the earth at about 66 degrees south of the equator.

Arctic Circle: the invisible ring around the northern part of the earth at about 66 degrees north of the equator.

atmosphere: all of the air surrounding a planet.

atom: the smallest particle of matter that cannot be broken down without changing the particle's properties.

biodegrade: to break down or decay and become absorbed into the environment.

biome: a large area inhabited by certain plants and animals that are well-adapted to the climate, geology, and water resources in the region.

birds of prey: birds that are predators.

buoyant: light and floating.

carbon dioxide: CO_2, a heavy colorless gas with molecules containing one carbon atom and two oxygen atoms. It is formed mostly by the combustion and decomposition of organic substances—such as when animals breathe and when animal and vegetable matter decays.

carbon footprint: the total amount of carbon dioxide and other greenhouse gases emitted over the full life cycle of a product or service, or by a person or family in a year.

carnivore: a creature that eats other creatures.

chlorofluorocarbons (CFCs): simple gases that contain carbon, chlorine, fluorine, and sometimes hydrogen, that are a major cause of stratospheric ozone depletion.

class: a group with common attributes; a major category in grouping organisms.

combustion engine: an engine that runs on heat, either from a furnace or from inside the engine itself.

community: all the living things within a region that interact with each other.

compost: a mixture produced by decomposing organic matter in a compost pile. Used to fertilize the soil in the garden.

coniferous: plants and trees that do not shed their leaves each year.

curvature of the earth: shape of the earth.

deciduous: plants and trees that shed their leaves each year.

decompose: to separate back down into its parts or elements.

dump: a place where waste is stored without being buried.

ecology: the interaction between organisms and their environment.

ecosystem: a community interacting with its environment, creating a working system.

ectotherm: an organism—like a snake—whose body temperature is affected by the environment.

El Niño: unusually warm ocean conditions occurring every few years along the tropical west coast of South America, which have dramatic effects on weather patterns around the world.

element: a simple substance made up of only one kind of atom, such as oxygen.

elevation: height above sea level.

environment: everything in nature—living and nonliving—including plants, animals, rocks, and water.

environmentalist: someone who works to preserve the environment.

equator: an invisible circle around the earth midway between the North and South Poles.

evaporate: to convert from liquid to vapor.

extinction: when a species no longer exists anywhere.

finite: something that is limited.

flora: plant life.

food chain: the feeding relationship between plants and animals in an environment.

food web: a community of organisms where there are several interrelated food chains.

fossil fuels: coal, oil, and natural gas.

geocaching: an outdoor treasure-hunting game using navigational techniques and clues to hide and seek containers called "geocaches" or "caches." A cache generally contains a logbook and "treasure," such as toys or trinkets.

geothermal: heated internally from the earth.

glacier: an enormous mass of ice and snow that moves slowly with the pull of gravity.

Global Positioning System: a system of satellites, computers, and receivers that can determine the exact location of a receiver anywhere on the planet.

global warming: an increase in the average temperature of the earth's atmosphere, enough to cause climate change.

glucose: the substance that makes up sugar crystals.

greenhouse effect: when the presence in the atmosphere of gases such as carbon dioxide, water vapor, and methane allow incoming sunlight to pass through, but absorb heat radiated back from the earth's surface, trapping solar radiation.

greenhouse gases: various gases, including water vapor, carbon dioxide, and methane, that absorb infrared radiation, trap heat in the atmosphere, and contribute to the greenhouse effect.

habitat: a plant or animal's natural "home," where it can find the food, shelter, and other conditions that are best suited to meet its needs.

hazardous waste: garbage that is dangerous to living beings.

helium: a light element, usually found in gases, and often used to inflate balloons.

herbivore: a creature that eats plant material.

homeotherm: an organism that can regulate its own body temperature.

hydrogen: the lightest and simplest element.

hydroponics: growing plants in nutrient solutions without soil.

kingdoms: divisions of living organisms into broad categories.

landfill: a place where waste and garbage is buried between layers of earth.

leaf litter: fallen leaves and other dead plant material that is starting to break down.

marine life: all organisms that live in the oceans.

meteor: a streak of light produced when a small particle from outer space enters the earth's atmosphere.

mid-latitudes: the areas between the equator and the North and South Poles.

molecule: the simplest structural unit of an element or compound. Molecules are made of atoms.

nocturnal: active at night.

Northern Hemisphere: north of the equator.

nuclear fusion: when hydrogen fuses into helium, producing energy and light.

organic: something that was part of a living thing.

organism: something living, such as a plant or an animal.

oxygen: the most abundant element on Earth, found in the air and in the water.

ozone depletion: the thinning of the ozone layer.

ozone: a gas that is a major air pollutant in the lower atmosphere but a beneficial part of the upper atmosphere. The ozone layer, which is located about 20 to 30 miles above the earth's surface, contains high levels of ozone that block most ultraviolet solar rays.

Glossary

persist: endure or not break down at all, even over time.

photosynthesis: the process in which plants use sunlight, water, and carbon dioxide to create energy.

phylum: a related group descended from a common ancestor.

plankton: the tiny plant and animal life that floats in bodies of water, such as algae, amoebas, and various larvae.

pollutant: any substance that pollutes, or dirties, the planet.

pollution: man-made waste that contaminates an environment.

precipitation: falling moisture resulting from condensation in the water cycle, in the form of rain, sleet, snow, etc.

predator: any animal that lives by preying on—eating—other animals.

radiation: very fast heat transfer.

salinity: the amount of salt in water or another liquid.

Santa Ana winds: Southern California winds that occur when air changes temperature moving over mountains.

savannah: an area with wide open, grassy areas and scattered trees.

sediment: material deposited by water, wind, or glaciers.

solar power: energy from the sun converted to electricity.

Southern Hemisphere: south of the equator.

species: a group of closely related and physically similar organisms.

subspecies: a division of a group of organisms from the main species.

subtropical: areas close to the tropics with weather that's usually very mild.

summer solstice: June 21 or 22, the day of the year when the Northern Hemisphere receives the most hours of daylight and the Southern Hemisphere receives the least.

sundial: a tool that uses a shadow cast by the sun to determine the time.

sustainable: continuing something with minimal long-term impact on the environment.

symbiosis: a close relationship between two different organisms in an environment.

temperate: areas of land that fall between the polar regions and the tropics, with different climates and biomes.

thermal vents: grooves in the earth's surface emitting very hot water heated from deep within the earth.

trade winds: a wind that blows almost continually toward the equator from the northeast north of the equator and from the southeast south of the equator.

turbine: a rotary engine, usually using a blade, that converts one type of energy to another.

ultraviolet: invisible radiation produced by the sun.

vapor: a substance suspended in the air as gas, like steam, mist, or fog.

vermicomposting: raising worms to break down organic materials.

vertebrate: organism with a backbone or spinal column.

vitamin D: a vitamin that is important for bones and teeth. It is found in egg yolks and milk, and it can be produced in the body from sunlight.

water cycle: the process where the planet's water evaporates, condenses, and returns to Earth.

wildlife refuge: an area of protected land where species can live away from human intervention.

winter solstice: December 21 or 22, the day of the year when the Northern Hemisphere receives the fewest hours of daylight and the Southern Hemisphere receives the most.

yellow dwarf: a small star, such as our own sun.

Books and Periodicals

Burton, Bob. *Endangered Environments!* Gareth Stevens Publishing, 1996.

Davies, Nicola. *Extreme Animals: The Toughest Creatures on Earth*. Candlewick, 2006.

Donald, Rhonda Lucas. *Endangered Animals*. Children's Press, 2002.

Gralla, Preston. *How the Enviroment Works*. Ziff-Davis Press, 1994.

Hoyt, Erich. *Extinction A–Z*, Enslow Publishers, 1991.

Kalman, Bobbie. *What are Food Chains and Webs?* Crabtree Pub. Co., 1998.

McCay, George. *The Encyclopedia of Animals: A Complete Visual Guide*. University of California Press, 2004.

Simon, Noel. *Nature in Danger: Threatened Habitats and Species*. Oxford University Press, 1995.

Simon, Seymour. *Earth: Our Planet in Space*. Simon & Schuster Children's Publishing, 2003.

Simon, Seymour. *The Sun*. HarperTrophy, 1989.

Sussman, Art. *Dr. Art's Guide to Planet Earth: For Earthlings Ages 12 to 120*. West Ed, 2000.

Tagliaferro, Linda. *Galapagos Islands: Nature's Delicate Balance at Risk*. Lerner Publications, 2001.

Thornhill, Jan. *This Is My Planet: The Kids' Guide to Global Warming*. Maple Tree Press, 2007.

Fun Web Sites for Kids

EPA Environmental Kids Club:
http://www.epa.gov/kids/

EEK (Environmental Education for Kids):
http://www.dnr.state.wi.us/eek/

National Geographic Kids:
http://kids.nationalgeographic.com/

EcoKids (Canadian site):
http://www.ecokidsonline.com/pub/index.cfm

US Dept. of Energy:
http://www.eere.energy.gov/kids/games.html

Earth Matters for Kids:

http://www.earthmatters4kids.org/main.html

Environmental Organizations and Websites Protecting the Environment

Conservation International
www.conservation.org
2011 Crystal Drive, Suite 500
Arlington, VA 22202

National Wildlife Federation
www.nwf.org
11100 Wildlife Center Drive
Reston, VA 20190

The Nature Conservancy
www.nature.org
Worldwide Office
4245 North Fairfax Drive, Suite 100
Arlington, VA 22203-1606

Sierra Club
www.sierraclub.org
National Headquarters
85 Second Street, 2nd Floor
San Francisco, CA 94105

World Wide Fund for Nature
www.panda.org
1250 24th Street NW
Washington, DC 20090-7180

Earthwatch Institute
www.earthwatch.org
3 Clock Tower Place, Suite 100
Maynard, MA 01754

Index

Index